Chocolate Mousse

And Other Fabulous Chocolate Creations

by
Betty Malisow Potter

A special thank you to Earl C. Potter Jr. and Brian Potter for all your help. You deserve the Chocoholic's Medal of Honor for tasting every recipe in this book! My appreciation to my friends, family and co-workers for their contributions of recipes, tasting expertise and moral support.

ISBN: 0-913703-11-7
First Printing, 1982
Second Printing, 1987
Third Printing, 1988
Fourth Printing, 1989
Fifth Printing, 1991
Sixth Printing, 1992
Seventh Printing, 1993

Coordinating Editor: Earl C. Potter Jr.

Published by New Boundary Concepts, Inc.
1389 Park Road
P.O. Box 848
Chanhassen, MN 55317

*For serious chocolate lovers only . . .
a treasury of the most devastatingly
delicious chocolate recipes imaginable.*

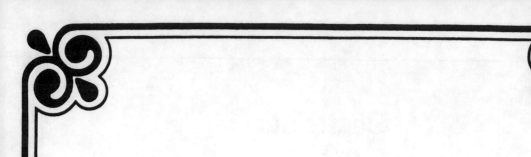

Dedication
To Earl Cullen, with my love

Contents

Chocolate Directory

Unsweetened Chocolate is natural rich chocolate that has no sugar added. It's made from ground cocoa beans that are processed. The resulting mixture is molded into 1-ounce squares and packed eight to a carton. Also called bitter, baking or cooking chocolate, it is used for all kinds of baking.

Semi-sweet Chocolate is unsweetened chocolate blended with additional cocoa butter and flavorings. It is processed with a low viscosity to make it more fluid when melted. It has a satin gloss.

Sweet Cooking Chocolate is similar to semi-sweet chocolate, but it contains a higher proportion of sugar. Also known as German sweet chocolate, it is packaged in 4-ounce bars and used in baking.

Milk Chocolate is referred to as eating chocolate and has dried milk added to it with a blend of other ingredients.

Unsweetened Cocoa Powder has no sugar added and by processing, most of the cocoa butter is removed. It is often used in baking because it blends so easily with dry ingredients. "Dutch process" is treated with an alkali and is darker in color and stronger in flavor.

White Chocolate (the chocolate that isn't) is made from cocoa butter or vegetable fats, but contains no cocoa.

Melting Moments

Chocolate burns easily so high heat is a formidable enemy. It causes chocolate to become dry and grainy, so never increase heat to speed melting. Use a double boiler and heat chocolate over hot, not boiling, water.

If you're in a hurry, chop or grate the chocolate first. If chocolate becomes grainy, rescue it by adding 1 tablespoon of solid vegetable shortening per pound (more if necessary) and stir until chocolate becomes fluid again.

Be sure utensils are perfectly dry. Even one drop of water can cause chocolate to thicken into a stiff mass. If this happens, stir in a small amount of solid vegetable shortening.

Unsweetened chocolate liquifies when melted. Semi-sweet, sweet cooking chocolate and milk chocolate will hold their shape when heated, until stirred.

Micro-Melt

Melting chocolate in the microwave oven is a great time saver. Instead of using a double boiler, place 2 to 3 ounces of chocolate in a microwave-safe dish. Microwave on high for 1 minute. Chocolate retains its shape when heated in the microwave, so remove and stir. Microwave for additional 30-second periods, stirring and testing until melted.

Chocolate Garnishes

"The finishing touch that turns good into glorious."

Chocolate Curls: Let a bar of chocolate stand in a warm place (80 to 85° F) until slightly softened. Using a vegetable peeler, carefully draw across chocolate bar using a slow smooth stroke until chocolate forms curl.

Chocolate Wedges: Melt 6 ounces semi-sweet chocolate or sweet cooking chocolate. Pour onto waxed paper-lined cookie sheet. Spread chocolate out to ⅛ to ¼-inch thick. Refrigerate until slightly hardened. Lift gently from waxed paper with spatula.

Chocolate Leaves: With a small brush, spread melted chocolate on the top of a fresh, washed, non-toxic leaf (mint, lemon, strawberry, rose, ivy). Place on waxed paper-lined cookie sheet and refrigerate. When hardened, carefully peel off leaf. Store in refrigerator until ready to use.

Chocolate Cut-Outs: Melt 6-ounces semi-sweet chocolate chips and 1 tablespoon butter. Pour onto waxed paper-lined cookie sheet, spreading ¼ to ⅛-inch thick. Chill until almost set. Cut with cookie cutters and lift gently off waxed paper with spatula.

Grated Chocolate: Take a cooled square or bar of any type chocolate and rub across a grater.

Shaved Chocolate: Use a vegetable peeler and scrape, using a short quick stroke, across a bar of any type chocolate.

Storing Chocolate

Store chocolate tightly wrapped in a cool, dry place at a temperature between 60° and 78°F. It is not recommended to store chocolate in the refrigerator, but in a warm climate, it may be necessary. If chocolate is refrigerated, it should be tightly wrapped so moisture doesn't condense on it and odors aren't absorbed. Let chocolate return to room temperature before using.

If chocolate becomes too warm, the cocoa butter in the chocolate will melt and rise to the surface, forming a dusty gray film called "bloom." This "bloom" is not harmful and does not affect the quality or flavor of the chocolate. When melted or used in baking, the chocolate will return to its original color.

Chocolate Substitutions

Ingredient Called For:	Substitution
1 square (1-ounce) unsweetened chocolate	3 tablespoons cocoa plus 1 teaspoon butter or vegetable shortening
6 ounces (1 cup) semi-sweet chocolate chips	2 ounces unsweetened chocolate plus 7 tablespoons sugar and 2 tablespoons shortening
Semi-sweet chocolate chips	The equivalent ounces of semi-sweet chocolate squares, chopped or melted
Pre-melted unsweetened baking chocolate	An equal amount of unsweetened baking chocolate

Chocolate Measurements

2 ounces chocolate chips	=	⅓ cup
3 ounces chocolate chips	=	½ cup
4 ounces chocolate chips	=	⅔ cup
6 ounces chocolate chips	=	1 cup
1 ounce unsweetened chocolate	=	1 square unsweetened chocolate
1 pound unsweetened cocoa powder	=	4 cups unsweetened cocoa powder

Cookies
&
Bars

Deep Dark Chocolate Fudge Cookies

"Like Mae West said, "Too much of anything is fantastic!"

7	ounces semi-sweet chocolate
2½	ounces unsweetened chocolate
3	tablespoons unsalted butter
1	cup sugar
3	eggs
1½	teaspoons strong brewed coffee
¾	teaspoon vanilla
¾	cup flour
½	teaspoon baking powder
¼	teaspoon salt
4	ounces semi-sweet chocolate, coarsely chopped
¾	cup chopped pecans

Melt 7 ounces semi-sweet chocolate, unsweetened chocolate and butter in the top of a double boiler; set aside. In a mixing bowl, beat sugar and eggs together until lemon colored; mix in coffee and vanilla. Gradually add flour, baking powder and salt, mix well. Stir in 4 ounces chopped semi-sweet chocolate and pecans.

Bake at 350° about 12 minutes until tops are shiny and cracked and cookies are soft to touch. Cool several minutes and remove to wire racks.

Chocolate Chip Cookies Supreme

*"Lavish amounts of chocolate and walnuts
combine to make an incredible cookie.
These are dedicated to Ruth Wakefield—We love you!"*

Makes 6 Dozen

1	cup vegetable shortening
½	cup butter or margarine, softened
1⅓	cups sugar
1	cup firmly packed brown sugar
4	eggs
1	tablespoon vanilla
1	teaspoon lemon juice
2	teaspoons baking soda
1½	teaspoons salt
1	teaspoon ground cinnamon
½	cup regular or quick cooking rolled oats
3	cups flour
2	(12 ounce) packages semi-sweet chocolate chips
2	cups chopped walnuts

In large bowl, beat shortening, butter, and sugars until light and fluffy (about 5 minutes). Add eggs, one at a time, beating well after each addition. Beat in vanilla and lemon juice.

continued

In another bowl, stir together baking soda, salt, cinnamon, oats, and flour. Beat into creamed mixture until well blended; stir in chocolate chips and nuts.

For each cookie, drop by tablespoonfuls, on a lightly greased baking sheet. Bake at 350° for 12–15 minutes or until golden brown. Transfer to racks and let cool.

The first chocolate chip cookie is thought to have originated in 1930 at the Toll House Inn in Whitman, Massachusetts. Ruth Wakefield added some chocolate to a shortbread batter hoping the chocolate would melt and she'd have chocolate shortbread. Millions of chocolate chip cookie fans are grateful for the bits of chocolate that did not melt!

Chocolate Chunk Cookies

"These are for the lovers of the thin, crispy type cookies."

Makes 4½ Dozen

1	cup butter or margarine, softened
¾	cup sugar
¾	cup light-brown sugar
2	eggs
1	teaspoon vanilla
1	teaspoon salt
2¼	cups flour
1	teaspoon baking soda dissolved in 1 teaspoon hot water
12	ounces semi-sweet chocolate, coarsely chopped
2	cups coarsely chopped walnuts or pecans

In a large mixing bowl, cream butter until fluffy. Gradually add sugars, creaming well. Add eggs, vanilla and salt, mixing until well blended. Stir in 1¼ cups of the flour and the baking soda mixture. Stir in remaining 1 cup flour, until just blended. Stir in chocolate and nuts.

Drop by tablespoonfuls onto foil-lined cookie sheets. Bake at 375° for 12 minutes or until lightly browned. Remove to wire racks to cool.

More Than A Chocolate Chip Cookie

"Loaded with chips, coconut, oatmeal, rice crispies and nuts."

Makes 6 dozen

1	cup butter, softened
1	cup vegetable oil
1	cup granulated sugar
1	cup brown sugar, packed
1	egg
½	teaspoon vanilla
½	teaspoon baking soda
½	teaspoon cream of tartar
½	teaspoon coconut extract
3½	cups flour
1	cut oatmeal
1	cup rice crispies
1	cup chopped nuts
12	ounces semi-sweet chocolate chips
½	cup grated coconut

Combine butter, oil, sugars, egg, vanilla, baking soda, cream of tartar and coconut extract in a large bowl; mix until well blended. Add flour, a cup at a time, until well blended. Fold in remaining ingredients.

Drop by tablespoonfuls onto an ungreased cookie sheet. Bake at 350° for 10 to 15 minutes or until golden brown. Let set a minute and remove to wire racks to cool.

Chocolate Chip Cookies

*"In a popularity poll, chocolate chip cookies ranked #1.
This recipe ranks with the best of them."*

Makes 4 dozen

⅓	cup solid vegetable shortening
⅓	cup butter or margarine, softened
½	cup granulated sugar
½	cup firmly packed brown sugar
1	egg
1	teaspoon vanilla
1½	cups flour
½	teaspoon soda
½	teaspoon salt
½	cup chopped walnuts or pecans
1	cup semi-sweet chocolate chips

Combine shortening, butter or margarine, sugars, egg and vanilla in large mixing bowl. Beat at medium speed until mixed thoroughly. In small bowl, blend together the flour, soda and salt; add to shortening mixture and mix well. Stir in nuts and chocolate chips.

Drop dough by rounded teaspoonfuls, about 2 inches apart, on ungreased baking sheet: Bake at 375° for 8 to 10 minutes, or until lightly browned but still soft. Cool on wire rack.

Chocolate Chip Oatmeal Cookies

"An old-fashioned favorite that's perfect to fill up the cookie jar."

Makes 5 Dozen

1	cup butter or margarine
6	ounces brown sugar
6	ounces white sugar
1	egg
1	teaspoon hot water
1	teaspoon vanilla
1½	cups flour
1	teaspoon baking soda
1	teaspoon salt
1	cup chopped pecans or walnuts
12	ounces semi-sweet chocolate chips
2	cups oatmeal

Cream butter and sugars together. Add egg, water and vanilla. Gradually add flour, baking soda and salt.

Stir in nuts, chocolate chips and oatmeal. Drop by tablespoonfuls on lightly greased baking sheet. Bake at 350° for 10 minutes. Remove to wire racks to cool.

Butter-Chip Cookies

"These buttery cookies are light and melt in your mouth."

Makes 25 Cookies

1	cup butter
1	cup powdered sugar
¼	teaspoon salt
1	teaspoon vanilla
2¼	cups flour
6	ounces semi-sweet chocolate chips or mini-chips
	Powdered sugar

Cream butter and 1 cup powdered sugar until well blended. Gradually add salt, vanilla and flour (mixture will be stiff). Stir in chocolate pieces.

Roll into 1-inch balls and place on ungreased cookie sheet. Flatten balls with fork. Bake at 350° for 12 to 15 minutes until set but not brown. While hot, sprinkle with powdered sugar. Remove to wire racks to cool.

Chocolate Marshmallow Cookies

"Moist chocolate cookies with a marshmallow layer and chocolate frosting."

Makes 3½ Dozen

1	cup brown sugar
1	egg, slightly beaten
½	cup milk
½	cup butter
2	(1-ounce) squares unsweetened chocolate
1½	cups flour
½	teaspoon baking soda
1	teaspoon vanilla
½	cup chopped pecans or walnuts
	Miniature marshmallows

Mix brown sugar and egg together; gradually add milk. Melt butter and chocolate together in a double boiler; add to milk mixture. Add flour, baking soda, vanilla and chopped nuts; mix thoroughly. Chill dough for 1 hour. Drop by tablespoonfuls onto a greased cookie sheet. Bake at 375° for 10 to 15 minutes. Take from oven and place 3 or 4 small marshmallows on each cookie, pressing in place. Return cookies to oven for a few seconds until marshmallows are slightly melted. Remove from cookie sheet and frost while still warm.

continued

Chocolate Frosting

2	(1-ounce) squares unsweetened chocolate
⅓	cup butter
1⅓	cups powdered sugar, sifted
1	egg
1	teaspoon vanilla

Melt chocolate and butter in a double boiler. Place in a bowl with the rest of the ingredients and mix well.

Chocolate Kiss Cookies

"A chocolate surprise is hidden inside each delectable powdery white ball."

Makes 3½ Dozen

1	cup butter
½	cup sugar
1	teaspoon vanilla
2	cups sifted flour
1	cup finely chopped pecans
1	(9-ounce) package milk chocolate kisses
	Powdered sugar

Cream butter, sugar and vanilla until light and fluffy. Add flour and nuts and mix until well blended. Put a scant tablespoon of dough around each kiss; roll between hands to make a ball shape. Place on ungreased cookie sheets. Bake at 375° for 12 minutes until set but not brown. Remove to wire rack, sprinkle liberally with powdered sugar.

HINT: To make the cookies chocolate, use 1¾ cups flour and ¼ cup unsweetened cocoa powder instead of 2 cups flour.

Chocolate Snaps

"Crispy, crunchy, chocolatey!"

Makes 4 Dozen

½	cup butter
1	cup brown sugar
1	egg, beaten
2	(1-ounce) squares unsweetened chocolate, melted
1	cup flour
½	teaspoon baking soda
¼	teaspoon baking powder
½	teaspoon salt
1	cup shredded coconut
1	teaspoon vanilla
1 ½	cups uncooked oatmeal
¾	cup semi-sweet chocolate mini-chips

Cream butter and sugar until well blended. Add egg and melted chocolate. Gradually add flour, baking soda, baking powder, and salt. Add coconut and vanilla. Stir in oatmeal and chips.

Drop by teaspoonfuls onto greased baking sheet. Flatten by criss-crossing with a fork. Bake at 350° for 20 minutes.

Chocolate Tipped Butter Cookies

"Beautiful for a party tray and perfect with coffee."

Makes 5 Dozen

1	cup butter
½	cup powdered sugar
1	teaspoon vanilla
2	cups flour
6	ounces semi-sweet chocolate chips
3	tablespoons butter
½	cup finely chopped pecans or walnuts

In a mixing bowl, cream 1 cup butter. Gradually add sugar, beating until light and fluffy. Blend in vanilla and gradually add flour until well mixed. Shape dough into 2½" long by ½" round logs. Place on ungreased cookie sheets. Flatten lengthwise with fork to ¼-inch thick.

Bake at 350° for 12 to 14 minutes. Cool on wire racks. Melt chocolate chips and 3 tablespoons butter in top of double boiler. Dip one end of cookie in warm chocolate to coat both sides. Roll in chopped nuts.

Chocolate Lace Cookies

"Lacy and candy-like, they're irresistible!"

½	cup butter
½	cup sugar
1	tablespoon flour
¼	teaspoon salt
¾	cup finely chopped almonds
2	tablespoons milk
1	teaspoon almond extract
3	(1-ounce) squares semi-sweet chocolate, melted

In a skillet, melt butter over medium heat. Add sugar, flour and salt; stir until sugar dissolves (about 3 minutes). Mix in almonds and milk; stir until slightly thickened. Remove from heat and stir in almond extract. Cool slightly and drop by teaspoonful, spacing 3 to 4 inches apart, on cookie sheets lined with foil (butter and flour foil). Bake cookies 5 to 7 minutes at 350° until light golden brown. Let stand 2 minutes and remove to rack to cool.

With a thin spatula, spread chocolate on the top of one cookie. Cover with flat side of another cookie to form a sandwich. Serve same day or may be frozen.

Cocoa Pretzels

"A slightly sweet cookie, beautifully shaped like a pretzel and dipped in (What else?) chocolate!"

Makes 3 dozen

¼	cup unsweetened cocoa powder
3	tablespoons hot water or coffee
½	cup butter
¼	cup sugar
2	cups flour
1	egg
1	teaspoon vanilla

Dissolve cocoa in hot water and let cool. In a mixing bowl, cream butter and sugar together until light and fluffy. Add cooled cocoa mixture and mix well. Gradually beat in flour. Mix in egg and vanilla until well blended.

Cover bowl and refrigerate for at least 30 minutes. Take about ¼ cup of dough and roll into a rope 12 inches long and ¼-inch wide. Shape ropes into pretzels and place on ungreased cookie sheets. Bake at 350° for 10 minutes. Cool and dip in glaze.

continued

Glaze

½   cup milk
½   cup light corn syrup
⅔   cup sugar
2   (1-ounce) squares unsweetened chocolate
2   (1-ounce) squares semi-sweet chocolate
1   teaspoon butter

Combine milk, corn syrup, sugar and chocolates in top of double boiler. Cook, stirring constantly, until sugar is dissolved and chocolate is melted. Stir in butter and remove from heat. Cool to room temperature.

Chocolate Loves

"A light and airy brownie flavor cookie with the crunch of nuts."

Makes 2 Dozen

2	large egg whites
½	cup sugar
6	ounces semi-sweet chocolate chips, melted
1¼	cups coarsely chopped walnuts or pecans

In a large bowl, beat egg whites until soft peaks form. Gradually add sugar until stiff and glossy. Fold in melted chocolate until blended; then fold in nuts.

Drop by heaping tablespoonfuls onto lightly greased cookie sheets. Bake at 350° for about 10 minutes until set and dry on top. Remove to wire racks to cool. Best served the day they are baked.

Can it be true? "Chocolate is Miracle Cure" *was the title of an article from the Globe. Authorities claim that chocolate (especially milk chocolate) can guard against tooth decay, lower blood pressure, help prevent heart attacks, ease arthritis pain, stave off bone deterioration, help dieting and best of all it boosts love-making powers.*

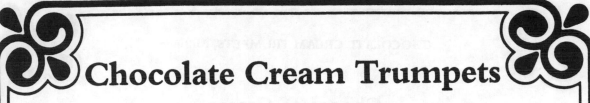

Chocolate Cream Trumpets

*"A French, rolled cookie, filled with Chocolate Cream—
absolutely worth the effort!"*

Makes 6 Dozen

¾	cup egg whites (6 to 8 eggs)
1⅔	cups granulated sugar
¼	teaspoon salt
¾	cup warm melted butter
¼	cup warm melted vegetable shortening
1	cup flour
¾	cup finely chopped almonds

In a mixing bowl, blend egg whites, sugar and salt until sugar is dissolved and mixture is thick (5 to 10 minutes). Slowly mix in butter and shortening. Stir in flour and almonds. Drop by scant teaspoonfuls onto greased and lightly floured baking sheets. Bake at 350° until edges are lightly brown. Quickly remove cookies and shape like cornucopias. Place cookies open-side down as they cool, so they will hold their shape as they harden. When cool, fill with Chocolate Cream.

continued

Chocolate Cream

½   cup butter, softened
5   egg yolks
⅓   teaspoon salt
⅓   cup milk
3   (1-ounce) squares unsweetened chocolate, melted
2   cups or more powdered sugar, sifted

In a mixing bowl, cream butter. Add egg yolks, salt and milk; beat until creamy. Stir in melted chocolate. Gradually add enough powdered sugar so frosting holds its shape but is not stiff or dry. Pipe chocolate into cookies with decorating tube or fill by dropping teaspoonfuls into cookie opening. If you wish, decorate ends of cookies by dipping them in nuts, coconut, powdered sugar, sprinkles, etc.

Chocolate Almond Balls

"A luscious powdery ball with the crunch of almonds and coconut."

Makes 7 Dozen

¾	cup butter
¾	cup solid vegetable shortening
2½	tablespoons cream cheese
⅔	cup powdered sugar
½	cup chocolate syrup
1	teaspoon vanilla
1	teaspoon almond extract
1	cup finely grated coconut
1	cup chopped almonds
3	cups sifted flour
¾	teaspoon salt
	Powdered sugar

Cream butter, vegetable shortening, cream cheese and ⅔ cup powdered sugar together. Mix in chocolate syrup, vanilla and almond extract. Stir in coconut and almonds.

Gradually add flour and salt, mixing until well blended. Chill for 1 hour or more until mixture is firm enough to roll into 1-inch balls.

Place balls on ungreased cookie sheets. Bake at 325° for 18 to 20 minutes. Cookies will not brown, but should hold their shape. While warm, roll in powdered sugar.

O'Chocolate Cookies

"A crunchy chocolate cookie wafer with a velvety chocolate frosting."

Makes 4 Dozen

½	cup butter
½	cup solid vegetable shortening
1½	ounces cream cheese
1	cup brown sugar
½	cup powdered sugar
2	eggs
2	(1-ounce) squares unsweetened chocolate, melted
2	teaspoons vanilla
2	cups sifted flour
1	teaspoon baking powder
½	teaspoon baking soda
½	teaspoon salt
1	cup chopped pecans or walnuts
1	cup oatmeal
¼	cup powdered sugar
	Chocolate Frosting (optional)

In a mixing bowl, cream butter, vegetable shortening, cream cheese, brown sugar and ½ cup powdered sugar together. Mix in eggs, melted chocolate and vanilla until well blended.

Gradually add flour, baking powder, baking soda and salt. Stir in nuts and chill for at least 1 hour.

continued

In a small bowl combine oatmeal and ¼ cup powdered sugar. Roll chilled dough into 1-inch balls and roll in oatmeal mixture. Place on greased cookie sheets.

Flatten with bottom of glass to ½-inch thick. Bake at 350° for 12 to 15 minutes. Cool and frost with Chocolate Frosting, if desired.

Chocolate Frosting

6	ounces (1 cup) semi-sweet chocolate chips, melted
1½	ounces cream cheese
1½	cups sifted powdered sugar
6 to 7	tablespoons cream

In a mixing bowl, blend chocolate, cream cheese and powdered sugar together. Add cream, a tablespoon at a time, beating until smooth and of spreading consistency.

Chocolate·Turtle Cookies

"Terrific tiny turtles."

Makes 4 Dozen

1	cup brown sugar
2	squares semi-sweet chocolate, melted
1	cup flour
¼	cup butter, melted
1	egg
½	pound pecan halves

Mix all of the ingredients together except pecans. For each cookie, place 4 pecan halves on a greased cookie sheet to form legs. Place a teaspoon of dough on pecans. Bake at 350° for 10 to 12 minutes. Cool on wire rack and frost.

Chocolate Frosting

2	squares unsweetened chocolate
⅓	cup butter
1⅓	cups powdered sugar, sifted
1	egg
1	teaspoon vanilla

Melt chocolate and butter together. Put chocolate mixture in a bowl with the rest of the ingredients and mix until well blended.

Chocadoodles

"The old favorite "snickerdoodles"
made even better with chocolate chips."

Makes 6 Dozen

1	cup butter, softened
1½	cups sugar
2	eggs
2¾	cups flour
2	teaspoons cream of tartar
1	teaspoon baking soda
½	teaspoon salt
¾	cup semi-sweet chocolate mini-chips
3	tablespoons sugar
1½	teaspoons cinnamon

In a mixing bowl, cream butter and 1½ cups sugar together until light and fluffy. Beat in eggs. Gradually add flour, cream of tartar, baking soda, and salt until well mixed. Stir in mini-chips and set aside.

In a small bowl, mix 3 tablespoons sugar and cinnamon together. Shape dough into 1-inch balls and roll in sugar mixture. Place 2 inches apart on ungreased cookie sheets. Flatten with a fork and bake for 8 to 10 minutes or until set. Remove to wire racks to cool.

Chocolate Mint Snaps

"Crispy, chocolatey, with a dash of mint."

Makes 10 Dozen

4	(1-ounce) squares unsweetened chocolate
1¼	cups shortening
2	cups sugar
2	eggs
⅓	cup corn syrup
2½	tablespoons water
2	teaspoons peppermint extract
1	teaspoon vanilla extract
4	cups flour
2	teaspoons baking soda
½	teaspoon salt
6	tablespoons sugar

Melt chocolate in double boiler; set aside. Cream shortening; gradually add 2 cups sugar until light and fluffy. Add melted chocolate, eggs, corn syrup, water and extracts; mix well. Add flour, baking soda and salt; mixing until blended.

Shape dough into 1-inch balls; roll balls in the 6 tablespoons sugar. Bake on ungreased cookie sheets at 350° for 10 minutes. Cool 5 minutes and remove to wire racks to cool.

The Ultimate Brownie

"So Rich—It should be listed on the Forbes 500!"

Makes 32 Bars

8	(1-ounce) squares unsweetened chocolate
1	cup butter
5	eggs
3	cups sugar
1	tablespoon vanilla
1½	cups flour
2½	cups chopped pecans or walnuts

Melt chocolate and butter in a saucepan over low heat; set aside. In a mixer, beat eggs, sugar and vanilla at high speed for 10 minutes. Blend in chocolate and flour just until mixed. Stir in nuts.

Pour into a greased 9 x 13-inch pan. Bake at 375° for 35 to 40 minutes (be careful not to overbake). Cool and frost if desired—but it is not necessary.

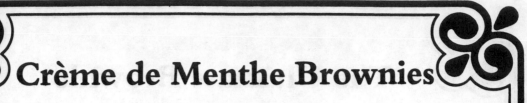

Crème de Menthe Brownies

"A sinful, sensuous, minty delight."

Makes 100 Small Bars

2	cups sugar
4	eggs, beaten
1	cup sifted flour
1½	cups chopped nuts
1	cup butter
4	squares unsweetened chocolate
½	teaspoon peppermint extract

Mix sugar, eggs, flour and nuts together. Melt butter and chocolate; add to other mixture. Add peppermint extract, blending well. Pour into greased jelly-roll pan. Bake at 350° for 20 to 25 minutes. Cool and frost.

Crème de Menthe Frosting

3	cups powdered sugar
4	tablespoons butter
3 to 4	tablespoons cream
2	teaspoons peppermint extract
	Few drops green food coloring

Mix powdered sugar, 4 tablespoons butter, cream, peppermint extract and green food coloring together. Beat until creamy and spread over cooled bars. Cover with chocolate icing.

continued

Chocolate Icing

4   tablespoons butter
4   (1-ounce) squares semi-sweet baking
         chocolate

Melt 4 teaspoons butter and chocolate together; stir until smooth; cool slightly. Spread over cream frosting.

Marbled Brownies

"Chocolate brownies with a swirl of cream cheese. Bring a batch to the office and earn some extra brownie points!"

Makes 20 Bars

4	ounces sweet baking chocolate
5	tablespoons butter
3	ounces cream cheese
1	cup sugar
3	eggs
½	cup plus 1 tablespoon flour
1½	teaspoons vanilla
½	teaspoon baking powder
¼	teaspoon salt
¼	teaspoon almond extract
¾	cup coarsely chopped nuts

Melt chocolate and 3 tablespoons butter in top of double boiler; set aside. Cream 2 tablespoons butter with cream cheese; gradually add ¼ cup sugar, beating until light and fluffy. Add 1 egg, 1 tablespoon flour, ½ teaspoon vanilla and mix well; set aside. In a separate bowl, beat 2 eggs; gradually add ¾ cup sugar, beating until well blended. Add baking powder, salt and ½ cup flour. Mix in melted chocolate, 1 teaspoon vanilla and almond extract. Stir in nuts.

Spread all but 1 cup chocolate batter in a greased 9-inch square pan. Pour cream cheese mixture on top. Drop remaining chocolate batter by tablespoons on top; swirl with a knife just to marble. Bake at 350° for 35 to 40 minutes.

Double Chocolate Brownies

"These brownies first appeared in <u>Recipes From Minnesota With Love.</u> They <u>had</u> to be included in this collection and should be listed in the Chocolate Hall Of Fame."

Makes 3 Dozen

4	squares unsweetened chocolate
1	cup butter or margarine
2	cups sugar
4	eggs
2	teaspoons vanilla
1	cup flour
	Pinch salt
1	12-ounce package semi-sweet chocolate chips
2	cups miniature marshmallows
	Powdered sugar

Melt unsweetened chocolate and butter together. Add sugar. Cool mixture. Add eggs, beating one at a time. Add vanilla, flour and salt; mix until well blended. Fold in chocolate chips and marshmallows.

Pour into a greased 9 x 13-inch pan. Bake at 350° for 30 to 35 minutes. Do not test for doneness. The top may look bubbly. Dust very well with powdered sugar.

Royal Brownies

"A brownie fit for a king, crowned with Buttercream Filling and Chocolate Frosting."

Makes 40 Bars

4	(1 ounce) squares unsweetened chocolate
1	cup butter
1	cup flour
¼	teaspoon salt
4	eggs
2	cups sugar
2	teaspoons vanilla
1½	cups chopped walnuts or pecans

Melt chocolate and butter in a saucepan over low heat; cool. Sift flour and salt together; set aside. In a mixing bowl, beat eggs until fluffy. Gradually beat in sugar until thick. Blend in chocolate mixture and vanilla. Fold in flour mixture until well blended. Stir in nuts.

Spread evenly in a greased 9 x 13-inch baking pan. Bake at 350° for 30 minutes or until firm. Cool and spread Buttercream Filling over top and frost with Chocolate Frosting.

Buttercream Filling

½	cup butter, softened
2	cups powdered sugar

continued

2   tablespoons golden rum
1   teaspoon vanilla
    Milk or more rum

Cream butter and powdered sugar together. Add rum and vanilla, beating until creamy. If necessary, add milk a teaspoon at a time, until smooth and creamy. Spread Buttercream Filling over cooled brownies. Spread Chocolate Frosting on top.

Chocolate Frosting

8   (1-ounce) squares semi-sweet chocolate
1   (3 ounce) white chocolate candy bar
1 to 2 tablespoons solid vegetable shortening

Melt semi-sweet chocolate in top of double boiler. Cool and spread over Buttercream Filling.

Melt white chocolate and 1 tablespoon shortening in top of double boiler. Cook and stir until melted and creamy. Add more shortening if necessary. Pour into pastry bag fitted with writing tip.

Pipe white chocolate in parallel lines, 1-inch apart, across length of pan. Take a knife and lightly draw it across the pan in the opposite direction at 1-inch intervals, to make checkerboard design over the top. Let stand until firm.

Meringue Brownies

"A brownie to brag about."

Makes 16 Bars

½	cup butter or margarine
2	(1-ounce) squares unsweetened chocolate
¾	cup sugar
1	egg
1	egg yolk
1	teaspoon vanilla
1	cup flour
½	teaspoon baking powder
1	egg white
½	cup brown sugar
¼	cup chopped walnuts or pecans

In a medium saucepan, melt butter and chocolate. Remove from heat; stir in sugar. Add egg, egg yolk and vanilla; mix well. Combine flour and baking powder and stir into chocolate mixture until blended.

Spread in a greased 8 x 8-inch pan. Beat egg white until soft peaks form. Gradually add brown sugar, beating until stiff peaks form. Spread meringue over batter. Sprinkle nuts over top. Bake at 350° for 30 to 35 minutes.

Caramel Brownies

"Zillions of calories—but who cares!"

Makes 24 Bars

1	German chocolate cake mix (dry)
½	cup plus 2 tablespoons butter or margarine, melted
⅔	cup evaporated milk
1	cup semi-sweet chocolate chips
1	(14-ounce) bag caramels
1	cup chopped pecans

Mix dry cake mix with butter and ⅓ cup of the evaporated milk. Pat half the dough into bottom of a 9 x 13-inch pan. Bake at 325° for 6 minutes.

Sprinkle chocolate chips over dough in pan. In a saucepan, heat caramels and remaining ⅓ cup evaporated milk; stir until creamy. Pour caramel mixture over chips and dough in pan.

Mix ½ cup of the chopped nuts into the remaining dough. Drop dough by spoonfuls over caramel mixture. Sprinkle remaining nuts on top. Bake at 325° for 18 to 20 minutes. Let sit until cool before cutting into bars.

Chocolate Meringue Bars

"Rich and Ritzy."

Makes 2 Dozen

½	cup butter
1½	cups brown sugar
½	cup white sugar
2	eggs, separated
1	teaspoon vanilla
2	cups flour
1	teaspoon soda
½	teaspoon salt
3	tablespoons water
¾	cup semi-sweet chocolate chips
¼	cup chopped pecans or walnuts

Cream butter, ½ cup of the brown sugar and the white sugar together until light and fluffy. Add egg yolks and vanilla. Sift flour, soda, and salt together. Add alternately to egg mixture with water, mixing well.

Press dough into a 9 x 13-inch pan. Sprinkle chocolate chips over dough. Beat egg whites until soft peaks form. Gradually add remaining 1 cup brown sugar until stiff. Spread over mixture in pan and sprinkle with nuts. Bake at 325° for 30–35 minutes. Cool and cut into bars.

Fudgy Rocky Road Bars

"Chocoholics rejoice! — These bars are scrumptious!"

Makes 48 Bars

Chocolate Layer

½	cup butter
2	(1-ounce) squares unsweetened chocolate
1	cup sugar
1	cup flour
1	cup chopped nuts
1	teaspoon baking powder
1	teaspoon vanilla
2	eggs

In a large saucepan, melt butter and chocolate. Add remaining ingredients and mix well. Spread in a greased and floured 9 x 13-inch pan. Top with filling.

Filling

6	ounces cream cheese, softened
½	cup sugar
2	tablespoons flour
¼	cup butter, softened
1	egg
½	teaspoon vanilla

continued

½	cup chopped nuts
1	cup semi-sweet chocolate chips
2	cups miniature marshmallows

In a bowl, combine cream cheese, sugar, flour, butter, egg and vanilla; mix until smooth and fluffy; stir in nuts. Spread over chocolate mixture. Sprinkle chocolate chips over top. Bake at 350° for 25 to 30 minutes or until toothpick inserted comes out clean. Remove from oven; sprinkle marshmallows over the top. Bake 2 minutes longer and frost immediately with Fudge Icing.

Fudge Icing

¼	cup butter
1	(1-ounce) square unsweetened chocolate
2	ounces cream cheese
¼	cup milk or cream
3	cups sifted powdered sugar
1	teaspoon vanilla

In a large saucepan, melt butter, chocolate, cream cheese and milk. Stir in powdered sugar and vanilla (add additional milk if too thick to pour). Immediately pour over marshmallow layer. Cool, cut into bars and store in refrigerator.

Cakes

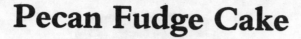

Pecan Fudge Cake

"Fabulous!"

Makes 10 Servings

¾	cup butter
¼	cup sugar
2¼	cups light brown sugar
2	eggs
3	(1-ounce) squares unsweetened chocolate, melted
1	teaspoon vanilla
2¼	cups cake flour
1½	teaspoons baking powder
½	teaspoon salt
1	teaspoon baking soda
1	cup milk
1½	cups chopped pecans

Cream butter and sugars together. Add eggs, beating well after each addition. Blend in chocolate and vanilla. Sift flour, baking powder, salt and soda together. Add flour mixture alternately with milk to chocolate mixture. Mix in nuts. Pour into three greased and floured 8-inch cake pans. Bake at 350° for 25 to 30 minutes. Cool and frost.

continued

Pecan Fudge Frosting

8	ounces cream cheese, softened
½	cup butter, softened
2–3	tablespoons milk
16	ounces powdered sugar
2	(1-ounce) squares unsweetened chocolate, melted
2	teaspoons vanilla
	Dash salt
1	cup chopped pecans

Beat cream cheese, butter and milk until well blended. Gradually add sugar; add more milk if necessary. Blend in chocolate, vanilla and salt. Frost cake and sprinkle pecans on top.

Chocolate Chiffon Cake With Chocolate Cream Center

"A Chocolate lover's delight—
chocolate cake with luscious chocolate cream."

Makes 12 Servings

Chocolate Chiffon Cake

7	large eggs, separated
½	cup unsweetened cocoa
¾	cup boiling water
1¾	cups sifted cake flour
1¾	cups sugar
1½	teaspoons baking soda
1	teaspoon salt
½	cup vegetable oil
2	teaspoons vanilla
½	teaspoon cream of tartar

Place egg whites in a large mixing bowl; set aside and let warm to room temperature. Place cocoa in a small bowl; stir in boiling water and let cool. In a separate bowl, mix flour, sugar, baking soda, salt, oil, vanilla, egg yolks and cocoa together until just blended; set aside. Sprinkle cream of tartar over egg whites. Beat with electric mixer at high speed until very stiff peaks form. Carefully fold batter into egg whites.

continued

Pour into an ungreased 10-inch tube pan. Bake at 325° for 1 hour or until top springs back when touched. Invert over neck of bottle; cool. Place cake on a serving plate. Cut a 1-inch slice across the top of the cake; set aside. Hollow out the center of the cake to form a cavity for filling; reserve the extra cake.

Chocolate Cream Filling

3	cups heavy cream
1½	cups sifted powdered sugar
¾	cup unsweetened cocoa
2	teaspoons vanilla
¼	teaspoon salt
1	teaspoon unflavored gelatin
2	tablespoons cold water

In a large mixing bowl, beat cream, sugar, cocoa, vanilla and salt until stiff peaks form; refrigerate. In a small saucepan, sprinkle gelatin over water to soften. Heat over low heat, stirring until gelatin is dissolved; cool.

Measure 2½ cups chocolate filling into a bowl. Fold in gelatin and use to fill cavity. Replace top. Mix ½ cup filling with reserved crumbled cake and use to fill center hole. Use remaining filling to frost top and sides of cake. Refrigerate until serving.

Black Forest Cherry Cake

"A classic cake with the taste of grand luxury."

Makes 12 Servings

6	eggs
1	cup sugar
½	cup flour
½	cup cocoa
1	teaspoon baking powder
½	teaspoon salt
½	cup plus 2 tablespoons butter, melted
1	teaspoon vanilla
3	tablespoon Kirsch

In a large bowl, beat eggs until thick; gradually add sugar, beating at high speed. Sift the next four dry ingredients together. Carefully fold dry ingredients alternately with melted butter into egg mixture. Stir in vanilla.

Pour into 2 greased and floured 9-inch round cake pans. Bake at 350° for 25 minutes or until done. Remove from oven and while still warm, sprinkle Kirsch over top. Let set 10 minutes and remove to wire racks to cool.

continued

Cream Frosting

2   cups whipping cream
1   tablespoon Kirsch
2   tablespoons sugar
1   (21-ounce) can cherry pie filling
         Glazed cherries or Cherry Cordials, garnish
         Chocolate curls, garnish

Whip cream; gradually add Kirsch and sugar until well blended. To assemble cake, place one cake layer on a serving plate. Spread half of cherry pie filling over cake. Cover with a thin layer of whipped cream.

Place second cake layer on top; spread remaining pie filling over cake. Cover with a thin layer of whipped cream. Frost sides and top with remaining whipped cream. Garnish with cherries and chocolate curls.

Chocolate Cheesecake

"Rich, smooth and supremely chocolate."

Makes 12 Servings

3	(8-ounce) packages cream cheese, softened
¾	cup plus 2 tablespoons sugar
3	large eggs
2	tablespoons sour cream
8	(1-ounce) squares semi-sweet chocolate, melted
1	teaspoon vanilla
2	tablespoons chocolate flavored liqueur
1	cup heavy cream

Beat cream cheese; gradually add sugar until smooth. Add eggs, one at a time, beating well after each addition. Beat in sour cream, chocolate, vanilla, chocolate liqueur and cream. Pour mixture into prepared pan. Take a sheet of heavy-duty aluminum foil and wrap it around bottom of pan to make waterproof seal. Set the pan in a larger pan and pour boiling water around it. Place in oven and bake at 375° for 1 hour and 15 minutes. Remove from water bath and let cool; chill 12 to 24 hours before serving. Garnish with additional whipped cream, chocolate shavings and almonds if desired.

continued

Chocolate Crust

2   cups chocolate wafer crumbs
½   teaspoon cinnamon
½   cup butter, melted

Mix wafer crumbs, cinnamon and butter together. Press onto bottom and sides of a 9-inch springform pan and chill.

Mocha Chill Cheesecake

"This chocolate temptation is especially good on a hot day."

Makes 12 Servings

1 ¼	cups chocolate wafer cookie crumbs
¼	cup sugar
¼	cup melted butter or margarine
12	ounces cream cheese, softened
1	(14-ounce) can sweetened condensed milk
⅔	cup chocolate flavored syrup
2	tablespoons instant coffee
1	teaspoon hot water
1	cup whipping cream, whipped
1	cup semi-sweet chocolate mini-chips

Mix cookie crumbs, sugar and butter together; pat crumbs on bottom and sides of a 9-inch springform pan and chill.

In a large mixing bowl, beat cream cheese until fluffy; add condensed milk and chocolate syrup, mixing well. In a small bowl, dissolve coffee in water and add to cream cheese mixture. Fold in whipped cream and chocolate chips; pour into prepared pan.

Cover with aluminum foil and freeze 6 hours or until firm. Garnish with additional cookie crumbs or grated chocolate or whipped cream.

Tuxedo Cheesecake

"A wonderful black and white creation—marbled chocolate and vanilla cheesecake with a chocolate crust."

Makes 12 Servings

Crust

2	tablespoons butter
1	cup chocolate wafer cookie crumbs
½	cup chopped pecans
12	(1-ounce) squares semi-sweet chocolate (used in crust and filling)
⅓	cup heavy cream (used in crust and filling)

Filling

1½	pounds cream cheese, softened
1¼	cups sugar
6	large eggs
½	cup heavy cream
¼	cup sour cream
1½	teaspoons vanilla

Butter bottom and sides of a 9-inch springform pan. Melt 1 tablespoon butter and add cookie crumbs to it. Press crumbs in bottom of springform pan; sprinkle with nuts.

continued

Melt chocolate in double boiler; stir in ⅓ cup cream and 1 tablespoon butter. Drizzle 3 tablespoons of chocolate mixture over nuts (reserve the rest for filling).

In a large bowl, beat cream cheese and sugar; add eggs one at a time. Blend in ½ cup heavy cream, sour cream and 1 teaspoon vanilla. Pour 3 cups of mixture into another container and add ½ teaspoon vanilla. Add reserved melted chocolate mixture to cream cheese mixture remaining in bowl.

Pour all but 3 to 4 tablespoons chocolate mixture over prepared crust. Pour vanilla layer over chocolate layer. Drop reserved chocolate by teaspoons over top. With a knife gently swirl to create a marbled effect.

Take a large sheet of heavy-duty aluminum foil, wrap it around the bottom of springform pan to make a waterproof seal. Place springform pan in a 9 x 13-inch pan and fill outer pan half full of water. Place in 300° oven and bake for 2 to 2½ hours until cheesecake is set. Cool; chill overnight and serve.

Chocolate Turtle Cake

*"A surprise layer of caramel and chocolate chips
between the layers of cake."*

Makes 16 Servings

1	German Chocolate cake mix
1	(14-ounce) bag caramels
1	(5-ounce) can evaporated milk
½	cup butter or margarine
1	(12-ounce) bag semi-sweet chocolate chips
1½	cups chopped pecans

Make cake mix according to package directions. Pour ½ batter in a greased 9 x 13-inch pan. Bake at 350° for 20 minutes.

In a saucepan, melt caramels, evaporated milk and butter together, stirring until creamy. While cake is still warm, pour caramel mixture over top.

Sprinkle chocolate chips and 1 cup of the chopped nuts over caramel mixture. Pour remaining batter on top and sprinkle remaining nuts over batter. Bake at 350° for 20 more minutes.

German Chocolate Cake Supreme

"A traditional favorite."

4	ounces German's sweet chocolate
½	cup boiling water
1	cup butter
2	cups sugar
4	eggs, separated
1	teaspoon vanilla
½	teaspoon salt
1	teaspoon baking soda
2½	cups flour
1	cup buttermilk

Melt chocolate in boiling water; cool. Cream butter and sugar until fluffy. Add egg yolks one at a time, beating well after each addition. Add melted chocolate and vanilla, mixing well.

Sift salt, soda and flour together and add alternately with buttermilk to chocolate mixture; beat until smooth. Beat egg whites until stiff and fold into chocolate mixture.

Pour into 3 greased and floured 8-inch cake pans. Bake at 350° for 30 to 40 minutes until cake tests done; cool and frost.

continued

Coconut-Pecan Frosting

1	cup evaporated milk
1	cup sugar
	Pinch salt
3	egg yolks
½	cup butter
1	teaspoon vanilla
1⅓	cups coconut
1	cup chopped pecans

In a saucepan, combine milk, sugar, salt, egg yolks and butter. Cook until melted and add vanilla. Continue cooking and stirring over low heat until thick (about 12 minutes).

Stir in coconut and pecans. Beat with a wooden spoon, until thick enough to spread. Frost cooled cake.

Hidden Giant Cupcakes

"A fabulous cupcake with chocolate chips and cream cheese hidden inside."

5 Dozen Miniature Cupcakes
or 18 Regular-Size Cupcakes

8	ounces cream cheese
1	egg
⅓	cup sugar
	Pinch salt
1½	cups semi-sweet chocolate chips
1½	cups flour
1	cup sugar
¼	cup unsweetened cocoa
1	teaspoon soda
½	teaspoon salt
1	cup water
1	tablespoon vinegar
⅓	cup vegetable oil
1	teaspoon vanilla
	Red maraschino cherries

Mix cream cheese, egg, sugar and salt until creamy. Stir in chocolate chips; set aside. Sift together flour, sugar, cocoa, soda and salt. Mix dry ingredients with water, vinegar, oil and vanilla.

continued

Divide cocoa mixture evenly into cupcake tins with liners. Put a spoonful of cream cheese mixture in the center of cocoa mixture. Garnish with ½ a cherry on large cupcakes, ¼ cherry on miniature cupcakes. Bake at 350° for 30 to 35 minutes for large cupcakes, 15 minutes for miniature cupcakes.

Texas Sheet Cake With Fudge Frosting

"Chocolate Pleasin' — Taste Ticklin' — Quick Fixin'."

Makes 15 Servings

2	cups flour
2	cups sugar
½	cup butter or margarine
½	cup vegetable oil
4	tablespoons unsweetened cocoa
1	cup water
½	cup buttermilk
1	teaspoon vanilla
1	teaspoon baking soda
1	teaspoon cinnamon
2	eggs, slightly beaten

In a large mixing bowl, blend flour and sugar together. In a saucepan bring to a boil, butter, oil, cocoa, and water. Gradually add cocoa mixture to dry ingredients. Blend in buttermilk, vanilla, baking soda, cinnamon and eggs. Pour into a greased 9 x 13-inch pan. Bake at 400° for 25 to 30 minutes.

continued

Fudge Frosting

½	cup butter or margarine
4	tablespoons unsweetened cocoa
5	tablespoons milk
16	ounces powdered sugar
1	teaspoon vanilla
1½	cups chopped nuts

In a saucepan, bring butter, cocoa and milk to a boil. Remove from heat; mix in powdered sugar and vanilla. Stir in nuts. Pour over cooled cake and let harden.

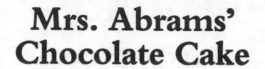

Mrs. Abrams'
Chocolate Cake

"Do you CRAVE a super chocolate cake?"
(Chocolate, Revered, Adored, Valued, Enjoyed)

Makes 8 Servings

2	cups sifted flour
1⅓	cups sugar
½	cup unsweetened cocoa
½	teaspoon salt
1	tablespoon baking soda
1	egg
⅔	cup vegetable oil
1	cup buttermilk
1	cup strong brewed coffee

Sift dry ingredients and place in mixing bowl. Add egg, oil and buttermilk. Mix until well blended. Add coffee and mix until just blended. Pour into 2 greased and floured 9-inch cake pans. Bake at 350° for 25 to 30 minutes, until cake springs back when touched. Cool and frost.

continued

Chocolate Frosting

3	tablespoons butter
2	ounces unsweetened chocolate, melted
3	cups powdered sugar
1½	teaspoons vanilla
2 to 3	tablespoons milk or brewed coffee

Mix thoroughly butter and cooled chocolate. Blend in sugar. Stir in vanilla and milk or coffee; beat until frosting is smooth and of spreading consistency.

Devil's Food Cake

"It's so rich and fudgy—who the devil cares about the calories?"

½	cup butter, softened
1	cup sugar
1	teaspoon vanilla
3	eggs, separated
2½	cups sifted cake flour
½	cup unsweetened cocoa powder
1½	teaspoons baking soda
1	teaspoon salt
1⅓	cups cold coffee
¾	cup sugar

Cream butter and 1 cup sugar until light and fluffy. Add vanilla. Add egg yolks, one at a time, beating well after each addition. Sift flour, cocoa, baking soda and salt together; add alternately with the coffee, beating well after each addition; set aside.

Beat egg whites to soft peaks form; gradually add the ¾ cup sugar, beating until stiff. Fold into batter until well blended. Pour into 2 greased and floured 8-inch cake pans. Bake at 350° for 35 to 40 minutes. Frost with Creamy Chocolate Frosting or a fluffy white frosting of your choice.

continued

Creamy Chocolate Frosting

¼	cup butter, softened
8	ounces cream cheese, softened
3	(1-ounce) squares unsweetened chocolate, melted
	Dash salt
3	cups sifted powdered sugar
⅓	cup half and half cream
1	teaspoon vanilla extract

Cream butter and cream cheese together. Mix in chocolate. Add salt and sugar alternately with cream, beating until smooth. Beat in vanilla. Frost cooled cake.

Double Chocolate Bundt Cake

"Chock-full of Chocolate."

Makes 12 Servings

1	cup butter
½	cup solid vegetable shortening
3	cups sugar
5	eggs
3	cups flour
½	teaspoon baking powder
½	cup unsweetened cocoa powder
½	teaspoon salt
1	cup milk
2	teaspoons vanilla
1½	cups chocolate chips
1	cup chopped walnuts or pecans

Cream butter, shortening and sugar together. Add eggs, one at a time, beating well after each addition. Add flour, baking powder, cocoa, salt, milk and vanilla; mix until well blended. Stir in chocolate chips and nuts.

Pour into a greased and floured bundt pan or angel food cake pan. Bake at 350° for 1 hour and 40 minutes. Dust with powdered sugar or frost with chocolate frosting, if desired.

Chocolate Chocolate Chip Banana Cake

"Old-fashioned goodness baked into every last mouthful."

Makes 15 Servings

½	cup butter
1½	cups sugar
2	(1-ounce) squares unsweetened chocolate, melted
2	eggs
2	cups cake flour
1½	teaspoons baking soda
1	cup sour cream
3	bananas, mashed
⅓	cup brown sugar
2	teaspoons cinnamon
1	cup chopped pecans or walnuts
6	ounces semi-sweet chocolate chips

In a mixing bowl, cream butter until fluffy; gradually add sugar mixing well. Mix in chocolate and eggs. Add flour and baking soda, alternately with sour cream. Mix in bananas. Pour half of mixture into a greased and floured 9 x 13-inch baking pan.

Mix brown sugar, cinnamon, nuts and chips together; sprinkle half of mixture over batter in pan. Add rest of batter; sprinkle with remaining sugar-nut mixture. Bake at 350° for 40 to 50 minutes until cake tests done.

Sugar 'n Spice Chocolate Cake

"Sugar 'n Spice, Chocolate, and Everything Nice."

Makes 20 Servings

2	cups sifted flour
3	tablespoons unsweetened cocoa powder
¾	teaspoon salt
½	teaspoon cinnamon
¼	teaspoon cloves
½	teaspoon nutmeg
¼	teaspoon allspice
¼	teaspoon baking soda
½	teaspoon baking powder
½	cup butter or margarine, softened
1½	cups sugar
2	large eggs
1	teaspoon vanilla
1½	cups (1 pound can) applesauce
1	cup semi-sweet chocolate chips
¾	cup chopped pecans or walnuts
	Chocolate Frosting (use Frosting for Texas Sheet Cake)

Sift flour, cocoa, salt, spices, soda and baking powder together; set aside.

continued

In a large mixing bowl, cream butter and sugar together. Add eggs, one at a time, and vanilla. Add flour mixture alternately with applesauce. Fold in chips and nuts.

Pour into a lightly greased 9 x 13-inch pan. Bake at 350° for 50 minutes until cake tests done. Cool and frost with Chocolate Frosting.

Lucious Ladyfinger Cake

"An exceptional dessert to be prepared a day ahead of time."

Makes 12 Servings

1	cup butter
3	cups powdered sugar
6	eggs, separated
3	squares unsweetened chocolate, melted
½	teaspoon almond extract
1	teaspoon vanilla
2	dozen ladyfingers, split
2	cups whipping cream
2	tablespoons powdered sugar
	Chocolate shavings, garnish
	Toasted almonds, garnish

Cream butter and 3 cups powdered sugar; add egg yolks, one at a time, beating well after each addition. Blend in melted chocolate, almond extract and vanilla; set aside. Beat egg whites until stiff and gently fold into chocolate mixture.

Line a 12-inch springform pan with ladyfingers. Spoon some of the chocolate mixture over ladyfingers. Alternate layers of chocolate and ladyfingers. Refrigerate overnight.

Before serving, whip cream with 2 tablespoons powdered sugar. Unmold cake and frost with whipped cream. Garnish with chocolate shavings and toasted almonds.

Chocolate Zucchini Cake

"A moist, tender cake, with an uncommonly good flavor."

Makes 12 Servings

¾	cup butter or margarine, softened
2	cups sugar
3	eggs
2½	cups flour
½	cup unsweetened cocoa powder
1	teaspoon salt
1	teaspoon cinnamon
½	cup milk
2	teaspoons vanilla
3	cups finely shredded zucchini
1	cup semi-sweet chocolate chips
1	cup chopped nuts
	Glaze or Cream Cheese Frosting

Cream butter and sugar together until fluffy. Add eggs, one at a time, beating well after each addition. Mix flour, cocoa, salt and cinnamon together. Add dry ingredients alternately with milk, beating until well blended. Mix in vanilla and zucchini. Stir in chips and nuts.

Pour into a greased and floured bundt pan. Bake at 350° for 50 to 60 minutes or until cake tests done. Cool for 15 minutes and remove cake from pan to finish cooling on wire rack. Cover with Glaze or frost with Cream Cheese Frosting.

continued

Glaze

2	cups sifted powdered sugar
3	tablespoons milk
1	teaspoon vanilla

Mix powdered sugar, milk and vanilla together blending until smooth. Pour over Chocolate Zucchini Cake while still warm.

Cream Cheese Frosting

6	ounces cream cheese, softened
½	cup butter or margarine, softened
2	teaspoons vanilla
4	cups sifted powdered sugar
	Milk

In a mixing bowl, beat cream cheese, butter and vanilla until light and fluffy. Gradually add the powdered sugar, beating until smooth. Add milk, if necessary, a teaspoon at a time, beating until smooth and creamy. Frost cooled cake.

Chocolate Walnut Fruitcake

"A very special fruitcake."

Makes a 3 pound fruitcake

2	eggs
1	cup sour cream
1	teaspoon vanilla
¼	cup butter, melted
1½	cups sugar
2	cups sifted flour
½	cup unsweetened cocoa powder
1	teaspoon baking soda
1	teaspoon salt
1	cup diced candied cherries
1	cup diced candied pineapple
1	cup raisins
1	cup chopped dates
2½	cups coarsely chopped walnuts
	Walnut halves, garnish

Mix eggs, sour cream and vanilla until well blended. Add butter and sugar, mixing well. Add flour, cocoa, baking soda and salt. Stir in candied fruit, raisins, dates and chopped walnuts.

Pour into a well greased 9-inch tube pan. Decorate top of cake with walnut halves. Bake at 300° for 1 hour and 45 minutes until cake tests done. Cool for 10 minutes and remove to wire rack to finish cooling.

continued

Store in a plastic bag, in a cool place, for at least a week before slicing. Can be stored for several months. Before serving, cut into thin slices.

HINT: For additional flavor and to insure its moist quality, brush cake from time to time with sherry, brandy, fruit juice, or apple cider (this is a great excuse to keep tasting the fruitcake). Another method is to saturate a piece of cheesecloth with sherry or brandy and wrap it around the cake before storing in plastic bag.

Chocolate Mousse Cake Roll

"Eight can blissfully polish off this little piece of heaven!"

Makes 8 Servings

8	ounces sweet baking chocolate
⅓	cup water
1	teaspoon Grand Marnier
8	eggs, separated
1	cup sugar
2	tablespoons cocoa
1	cup whipping cream
3	tablespoons powdered sugar
½	teaspoon vanilla extract
6	ounces semi-sweet chocolate chips
	Whipped cream, garnish
	Chocolate curls, garnish

Grease bottom and sides of an 18 x 12 x 1-inch jellyroll pan with vegetable oil. Line the greased pan with waxed paper. In a double boiler, melt sweet baking chocolate and water. Stir in Grand Marnier and let cool. In a large bowl, beat egg yolks until foamy. Gradually add 1 cup sugar until thick and lemon colored. Mix in chocolate mixture; set aside. Beat egg whites (at room temperature) until stiff; fold gently into chocolate mixture. Pour into jellyroll pan. Bake at 350° for 20 minutes.

continued

Remove from oven and immediately cover with damp paper towel; let cool 20 minutes. Carefully remove towel and sift cocoa on top. Invert pan over waxed paper; peel paper from cake. Beat whipping cream until foamy; gradually add powdered sugar and vanilla, beating until soft peaks form. Spoon evenly over cake. Start at short side and roll up the cake. Carefully slide cake seam-side down on serving plate. Melt chocolate chips and pour over cake. Chill cake and trim ends from cake roll. Garnish with whipped cream and chocolate curls.

Fudge Ribbon Cake

"A blue-ribbon chocolate cake with a cream cheese layer and chocolate frosting."

Makes 12 Servings

2	cups flour
2	cups sugar
1	teaspoon salt
1	teaspoon baking powder
½	teaspoon baking soda
1⅓	cups milk
½	cup butter, softened
2	eggs
4	(1-ounce) squares unsweetened chocolate, melted
1	teaspoon vanilla
	Cream Cheese Batter
	Chocolate Frosting

Sift together flour, sugar, salt, baking powder, and baking soda; set aside. In a mixing bowl, blend 1 cup of the milk and butter. Add eggs, one at a time. Add chocolate, flour mixture, remaining ⅓ cup milk and vanilla; beat until well blended.

Spread half of chocolate mixture in a greased bundt pan. Pour Cream Cheese Batter over and cover with remaining chocolate mixture. Bake at 350° for 50 to 60 minutes until cake tests done. Cool and frost with Chocolate Frosting.

continued

Cream Cheese Batter

1	(8-ounce) package cream cheese
¼	cup sugar
2	tablespoons butter
1	tablespoon cornstarch
1	egg
2	tablespoons milk
½	teaspoon vanilla

Blend cream cheese, sugar, butter, and cornstarch until creamy. Add egg, milk, and vanilla; mix until smooth.

Chocolate Frosting

¼	cup milk
¼	cup butter, softened
2	(1-ounce) squares unsweetened chocolate, melted
1	teaspoon vanilla
2½	cups powdered sugar, sifted

In a saucepan, bring milk and butter to a boil. Blend in chocolate and vanilla. Stir in powdered sugar until smooth.

Chocolate Feather Cake

"Aunt Florence Levine is a wonderful cook and this is one of her specialties."

Makes 2 (8-inch) Layers

½	cup butter or margarine
2	cups sifted self-rising flour
½	teaspoon baking soda
1	cup sugar
1	cup milk
2	(1-ounce) squares unsweetened chocolate, melted
2	eggs
1	teaspoon vanilla

In a mixing bowl, cream butter or margarine until fluffy. Sift in flour, baking soda and sugar. Add ¾ cup of the milk and beat 2 minutes at medium speed.

Blend in chocolate, eggs, vanilla and ¼ cup milk. Beat 2 minutes and pour into 2 greased and wax paper-lined 8-inch cake pans.

Bake at 350° for 25 to 30 minutes until cake tests done. Cool and frost with Feather Frosting and drizzle Chocolate Icing in a circle around top of cake so icing dribbles down the sides.

continued

Feather Frosting

2	cups sugar
¾	cup water
1	tablespoon light corn syrup or
	¼ teaspoon cream of tartar
	Dash salt
2	egg whites
1	teaspoon vanilla

In a saucepan, cook sugar, water, corn syrup and salt over low heat until sugar dissolves. Let pan sit 2 to 3 minutes (to let sugar crystals on sides of pan dissolve). Continue cooking to soft ball stage (240°).

In a mixing bowl, beat egg whites until stiff. Gradually add hot syrup to egg whites, beating constantly. Add vanilla and continue beating until spreading consistency (about 6 minutes).

Chocolate Icing

4	ounces sweet cooking chocolate
1	egg, slightly beaten

In double boiler, melt chocolate and stir in egg until well blended. Drizzle over Feather Frosting in a circle around the top of cake so it drips down the sides.

Pies

Chocolate Heaven
Walnut Pie

"It's just as rich and wonderful as it sounds."

Makes 8 Servings

1	cup unsalted butter, softened
1	cup light brown sugar
4	teaspoons unsweetened cocoa powder
2	teaspoons vanilla
3	(1-ounce) squares unsweetened chocolate, melted
4	eggs
1	cup chopped, roasted walnuts
	Chocolate Walnut Crust (recipe follows)
	Chocolate Mocha Cream (recipe follows)

In a mixing bowl, cream butter until light and fluffy. Beat in sugar, cocoa powder and vanilla until smooth. Stir in melted chocolate. Add eggs one at a time, beating very well after each addition. Sprinkle walnuts over cooled crust; mound filling into crust. Chill several hours; top with Chocolate Mocha Cream before serving.

continued

Chocolate Walnut Crust

1	cup flour
¼	cup light brown sugar
¼	teaspoon salt
6	tablespoons chilled butter
⅓	cup finely chopped walnuts
3	tablespoons finely chopped unsweetened chocolate
1	tablespoon cold water (may have to add more)
1	teaspoon vanilla

Combine flour, sugar and salt in a large bowl. Cut in butter until crumbly. Stir in walnuts and chocolate. Blend in water and vanilla, stirring with a fork until pastry holds together and leaves sides of bowl. Press mixture into a 9-inch pie plate. Bake at 350° for 15 to 20 minutes until lightly browned.

continued

Chocolate Mocha Cream

1	cup whipping cream
1½	tablespoons unsweetened cocoa powder or instant coffee powder
¼	cup powdered sugar
	Grated semi-sweet chocolate, garnish

Whip cream until soft peaks form. Add cocoa and sugar gradually until stiff peaks form. Pipe with pastry bag or mound with a spoon on pie; garnish with grated chocolate.

Succulent Chocolate Mousse Pie

"You'll need a springform pan and 8 avowed chocolate lovers!"

Makes 8 Servings

8	eggs, separated
1½	cups sugar
2	teaspoons vanilla
¼	teaspoon salt
½	cup brandy
10	ounces unsweetened chocolate
2.	ounces semi-sweet chocolate
¾	cup butter, softened
½	cup brewed coffee
3	tablespoons sugar
1½	cups whipping cream, whipped
	Chocolate crust
	Whipped cream, garnish
	Chocolate shavings, garnish

In a double boiler, cook egg yolks, 1½ cups sugar, vanilla, salt and brandy over simmering water. Beat mixture until pale yellow and thick (8 to 10 minutes); set aside. Melt chocolates and gradually beat butter into it. Gradually beat chocolate mixture into egg yolk mixture until very thick; beat in coffee.

continued

Beat egg whites (at room temperature) until soft peaks form. Gradually add 3 tablespoons sugar until stiff. Gradually fold egg whites into chocolate mixture until thoroughly blended. Gently fold in whipped cream. Pour into chocolate crust and refrigerate overnight. Garnish with additional whipped cream and chocolate shavings.

Chocolate Crust

1½   cups chocolate wafer crumbs
3   tablespoons butter, melted

Mix crumbs and butter and press into bottom of a 9-inch springform pan. Bake at 325° for 10 minutes; cool.

Chocolate-Nut Angel Pie

"Satisfy your chocolate passion with heavenly perfection."

8 Servings

Meringue Crust

½   cup sugar
⅛   teaspoon cream of tartar
2   egg whites
½   cup chopped pecans

Sift sugar and cream of tartar. Beat egg whites until stiff. Add sifted sugar gradually to the egg whites, beating well after each addition. Continue beating until the meringue is quite stiff and no sugar crystals are present. Fold in nuts.

Pour into well greased 9-inch pie plate. Bake in slow oven at 275° for 1 hour or until delicately browned. Cool thoroughly.

continued

Chocolate Filling

¾   cup semi-sweet chocolate chips
3   tablespoons hot water
1   teaspoon vanilla
1   cup heavy cream

Melt chocolate chips in top of double boiler. Add hot water and cook until thick. Cool slightly and add vanilla. Whip cream and fold it into chocolate. Pour into meringue shell and chill 2 to 3 hours.

Fudge Pecan Pie

"An intense, fudgy, pecan pie topped with whipped cream."

Makes 8 Servings

4	ounces semi-sweet chocolate pieces
2	(1-ounce) squares unsweetened chocolate
3	tablespoons butter
1	cup light corn syrup
¾	cup sugar
3	eggs
½	teaspoon salt
1	teaspoon vanilla
1	cup chopped pecans
1	prepared 9-inch pie crust, unbaked
	Whipped cream, garnish

Melt chocolates and butter together in top of double boiler. In a saucepan, simmer corn syrup and sugar for 2 minutes; stir in chocolate mixture and cool.

In a mixing bowl, blend eggs and salt together. Slowly add syrup mixture to eggs until well blended. Mix in vanilla and nuts. Pour into pie crust and bake at 325° for 35 minutes. Cool and serve with whipped cream.

Black Bottom Pie

"One of those desserts never to be forgotten!"

Makes 8 Servings

1	tablespoon unflavored gelatin
¼	cup water
2	(1-ounce) squares semi-sweet chocolate
½	cup sugar
2	tablespoons flour
2	cups scalded milk
3	egg yolks, well beaten
1	prepared 9-inch pie crust
¼	teaspoon salt
1	tablespoon rum or rum flavoring
3	egg whites
¼	teaspoon cream of tartar
¼	cup sugar
	Whipped cream, garnish
1	tablespoon powdered sugar
	Shaved chocolate, garnish
	Chopped pecans, garnish

continued

In a small bowl, sprinkle gelatin over water to soften; set aside. Melt chocolate in top of double boiler; set aside. Combine ½ cup sugar and flour in saucepan; gradually add scalded milk; stirring constantly over medium heat until thick (about 5–8 minutes). Remove mixture from heat. Add egg yolks and mix well. Remove 1 cup of the custard and stir into melted chocolate until well blended; pour into the pie crust. Pour gelatin into remaining hot custard. Stir in salt and rum; set aside to cool.

In a mixing bowl, beat egg whites with cream of tartar until fluffy; gradually add ¼ cup sugar. Fold into cooled custard. Spoon over chocolate mixture in the pie crust. Chill for 3 hours. Whip cream and powdered sugar together. Pipe around pie to form a ring. Garnish with shaved chocolate and top with pecans.

Mint Pie in
Double Chocolate Crust

"Cool, minty and refreshing."

Makes 8 Servings

1	envelope unflavored gelatin
1	cup cold water
½	cup sugar
⅛	teaspoon salt
3	eggs, separated
½	teaspoon peppermint extract
	Few drops green food coloring
1	cup whipping cream, whipped
	Double chocolate crust

In a saucepan, sprinkle gelatin over water to soften. Add ¼ cup sugar, salt and egg yolks; stir until blended. Cook over low heat, stirring constantly until mixture thickens slightly (about 5 minutes). Remove from heat, stir in extract and food coloring. Chill mixture, stirring occasionally, until mixture mounds slightly when dropped from spoon.

Beat egg whites until stiff but not dry. Gradually add remaining ¼ cup sugar and beat until stiff and glossy. Fold in gelatin mixture. Fold in whipped cream. Pour into Double Chocolate Crust and chill.

continued

Double Chocolate Crust

6	ounces semi-sweet chocolate chips
1	teaspoon vegetable shortening
	About 2 dozen chocolate cookie wafers
	Whipped cream, garnish

In top of double boiler melt chocolate and shortening. Spread tops of 11 wafers with melted chocolate; place on waxed paper-lined cookie sheet; chill. Spread chocolate half way down back of wafers; chill again. Spread tops of 7 additional wafers with melted chocolate and set in bottom of 9-inch pie plate.

Crush some wafers to fill up spaces on bottom of pie plate; chill. When chocolate is firm, line up the 11 cookies around edge of pie plate so that frosted backs stick up over the rim of the plate. Fill pie shell with peppermint filling. Garnish with whipped cream and additional cookie crumbs sprinkled on top. Chill until ready to serve.

Chocolate Velvet Strawberry Tart

*"If you have a passion for chocolate and strawberries
. . . look no further."*

Makes 8 Servings

Tart Shell

1⅔	cups flour
¼	cup sugar
½	teaspoon salt
½	cup plus 2 tablespoons unsalted butter
2	egg yolks, slightly beaten
1	teaspoon vanilla
2	teaspoons cold water

Sift flour, sugar and salt into a mixing bowl. Cut in butter with
a pastry blender or fork until it resembles coarse meal. With a
fork, blend in yolks, vanilla and water. Shape into a ball; knead
with palm of hand several times and reshape into ball. Chill 2
to 3 hours. Roll out between waxed paper and fit into bottom
and sides of an 8-inch tart pan; prick with fork and chill for 1
hour. Fit a piece of aluminum foil inside tart pan, covering
crust. Sprinkle with dry beans to weigh down crust. Bake at
425° for 8 to 10 minutes until light brown.

continued

Chocolate Velvet Filling

1	cup semi-sweet chocolate chips
2	tablespoons butter, melted
3	tablespoons Kirsch
¼	cup sifted powdered sugar
1	tablespoon water

Melt chocolate in top of double boiler. Wisk in butter and Kirsch. Gradually add sugar and water until well blended. While still warm, pour into tart shell.

Fresh Strawberries and Glaze

1½	pints strawberries, washed, dried and sliced in half
3	tablespoons red currant jelly
1	tablespoon Kirsch
	Whipped cream, garnish
	Chocolate shavings, garnish

Layer strawberries in a circular pattern over chocolate filling. In a small saucepan, heat jelly and Kirsch together, stirring until blended.

Brush over berries. Refrigerate for 2 to 4 hours; garnish with whipped cream and chocolate shavings and serve.

Chocolate Chiffon Pie

"Light and fluffy like a chocolate cloud."

Makes 8 Servings

1 envelope unflavored gelatin
¼ cup cold water
1¼ cups milk
2 (1-ounce) squares unsweetened chocolate
¼ cup plus 2 tablespoons sugar
¼ teaspoon salt
3 eggs, separated
1 teaspoon vanilla
   Chocolate crumb crust
   Whipped cream, garnish
   Chocolate curls, garnish

In a small bowl, sprinkle gelatin over cold water; let soften. In the top of a double boiler, heat milk and chocolate until melted. Add ¼ cup sugar, salt and slightly beaten egg yolks; cook until thick (do not boil). Remove from heat and stir in gelatin until dissolved. Chill until mixture mounds when dropped from spoon. Beat egg whites until soft peaks form; gradually add 2 tablespoons sugar and vanilla, beating until stiff peaks form. Gently fold into chocolate mixture until blended. Spoon into chocolate crumb crust. Chill several hours before serving. Garnish with whipped cream and chocolate curls.

continued

Chocolate Crumb Crust

1½	cups chocolate wafer crumbs
¼	cup sugar
2	teaspoons instant coffee powder (optional)
½	cup melted butter

Mix ingredients together and press evenly onto bottom and sides of 9-inch pie plate. Bake at 350° for 10 minutes. Cool crust and fill.

White Chocolate Silk Pie

"An exquisite dessert."

Makes 8 Servings

½   pound butter, melted
2   ounces good quality white chocolate, melted
1   cup powdered sugar
4   eggs
½   teaspoon vanilla
     Prepared chocolate crust (see Chocolate Mint Pie)
     Whipped cream, garnish
     Toasted almonds, garnish

In a mixing bowl, combine butter and chocolate together. Gradually add powdered sugar until well mixed. Add eggs, one at a time, beating very well after each addition. Add vanilla and beat until thick.

Pour into prepared pie crust and refrigerate several hours or overnight. Garnish with whipped cream and toasted almonds.

Note: The filling can also be prepared and served in individual serving dishes.

French Silk Pie

"Heavenly, melt-in-your-mouth, silky chocolate."

8 Servings

1	baked 9-inch pie shell
¾	cup powdered sugar
¼	pound butter
¼	pound semi-sweet chocolate
½	teaspoon vanilla
3	eggs
	Whipped cream, garnish
	Chocolate shavings, garnish

Cream sugar and butter, blending very well. Melt chocolate in double boiler and beat into mixture. Add vanilla. Add eggs, one at a time, beating well after each addition at high speed.

Pour into pie shell. Refrigerate several hours. When ready to serve, garnish with whipped cream and chocolate shavings.

Chocolate Banana Rum Pie

"A creamy classic with a delicious twist."

Makes 6 Servings

Meringue Crust

3	egg whites
½	teaspoon baking powder
1	cup sugar
1	teaspoon vanilla
½	teaspoon almond extract
2	medium bananas

Beat egg whites until foamy. Add baking powder and beat until egg whites stand in soft peaks. Gradually add sugar, beating until egg whites are stiff. Stir in vanilla and almond extract.

Spread meringue over bottom of a greased 9-inch pie pan, spreading edge up along sides of pan. Bake at 300° for 35 to 45 minutes. Remove from oven, and cool. Slice bananas into shell. Spread Chocolate Rum Filling over bananas. Refrigerate.

continued

Chocolate Rum Filling

1	cup semi-sweet chocolate chips
1	cup whipping cream
3	tablespoons rum
¼	cup finely chopped almonds, optional
	Whipped cream, garnish
	Chocolate curls, garnish

Melt chocolate in top of double boiler; set aside. Whip cream until stiff. Fold rum and almonds into whipped cream and blend in chocolate. Spread over bananas in pie shell. Garnish with whipped cream and chocolate curls.

Rocky Road Fudge Pie

"For those who love that combination of chocolate, marshmallows and nuts."

Makes 8 Servings

½	cup butter
½	cup sugar
2	eggs
2	(1-ounce) squares unsweetened chocolate, melted and cooled
1	teaspoon vanilla
1	cup miniature marshmallows
½	cup chopped walnuts, optional
1	prepared 9-inch chocolate crust (see Chocolate Mint Pie)
	Whipped cream, garnish
	Chocolate shavings, garnish

Cream butter and sugar. Add eggs, one at a time, beating well after each addition. Add chocolate and vanilla; beat until fluffy. Fold in marshmallows and walnuts.

Spoon into prepared crust. Chill several hours until firm. Garnish with whipped cream and chocolate shavings.

Chocolate Ripple Eggnog Pie

*"A swirl of chocolate runs through a luscious rum
and eggnog filling."*

Makes 8 Servings

¼	cup cold water
1	envelope (1 tablespoon) unflavored gelatin
2	tablespoons cornstarch
½	cup sugar
2	cups prepared eggnog
1½	ounces semi-sweet chocolate
1	cup whipping cream
3 to 6	tablespoons rum or ¾ teaspoon rum flavoring
	Chocolate crust
	Whipped cream, garnish
	Chocolate curls, garnish

Pour water into a small bowl and sprinkle with gelatin; set
aside. In a pan over medium heat, stir together cornstarch,
sugar and eggnog. Cook, stirring until thickened; stir in
gelatin. Divide mixture in half and stir melted chocolate into
one portion. Refrigerate both portions until thick but not set.

continued

In a bowl, beat whipping cream until soft peaks form. Fold whipped cream and rum into white portion; then spoon into Chocolate Crust. Spoon chocolate portion over top. With a knife, gently swirl chocolate through cream layer. Refrigerate at least 4 hours or overnight. Garnish with whipped cream and chocolate curls.

Chocolate Crust

1	cup flour
¼	cup brown sugar
¾	cup chopped pecans or walnuts
1	(1-ounce) square semi-sweet chocolate, grated
⅓	cup butter, melted

Mix flour, brown sugar, nuts and chocolate together. Stir in butter and mix well. Press into bottom and sides of 9-inch pie plate. Bake at 375° for 15 minutes or until light brown; cool.

German Sweet Chocolate Pie

"Nothing can top this pie except a dollop of whipped cream."

4	ounces sweet cooking chocolate
¼	cup butter
1	(13-ounce) can evaporated milk
1	cup sugar
⅛	teaspoon salt
3	eggs
1	teaspoon vanilla
1	prepared 10-inch pie shell
1⅓	cups grated coconut
½	cup chopped pecans
	Whipped cream, garnish
	Chocolate shavings, garnish

Melt chocolate with butter over low heat, stir until blended. Remove from heat and gradually blend in milk; set aside. In a mixing bowl combine sugar, and salt. Beat in eggs and vanilla. Gradually blend in chocolate mixture.

Pour into pie shell. Mix coconut and pecans together; sprinkle over filling. Bake at 375° for 45 minutes or until top is puffed (filling will be soft, but will set while cooling). Cool at least 4 hours before serving. Garnish with whipped cream and chocolate shavings.

Fudge Peppermint
Ribbon Pie

*"A fudge and peppermint ice cream pie with a peppermint meringue
—it's beautiful at holiday time."*

2	tablespoons butter
2	(1 ounce) squares unsweetened chocolate
1	cup sugar
⅔	cup evaporated milk
1	teaspoon vanilla
1	quart pink peppermint ice cream, softened
1	(9-inch) baked and cooled chocolate crumb crust

To make fudge sauce, combine the butter, chocolate, sugar, and evaporated milk in a heavy saucepan. Cook and stir until mixture is thick and bubbly and chocolate is melted. Stir in vanilla and cool. Spread two cups of softened ice cream in pie shell. Cover with half the cooled fudge sauce; freeze until firm. Repeat with layer of ice cream and fudge sauce. Freeze several hours or overnight until firm. When ready to serve, make Peppermint Meringue and spread over pie.

continued

Peppermint Meringue

3	egg whites
½	teaspoon vanilla
¼	teaspoon cream of tartar
6	tablespoons sugar
4	tablespoons crushed peppermint candy

Beat egg whites with vanilla and cream of tartar to form soft peaks. Gradually add sugar beating until stiff peaks form. Fold in 3 tablespoons of the crushed candy. Spread meringue over frozen pie, seal to edge. Sprinkle with 1 tablespoon crushed candy. Bake at 475° for 5 minutes, until meringue is golden.

Mile High Chocolate Chill Pie

"Fattening, intoxicating, gorgeous."

Makes 8 Servings

1	pint pistachio or coffee ice cream
1	pint chocolate chocolate chip ice cream
1	baked pie shell or chocolate crust (See Chocolate Chiffon Pie)
8	egg whites (room temperature)
¼	teaspoon cream of tartar
½	cup sugar
½	teaspoon vanilla

Put a layer of pistachio ice cream in bottom of pie shell. Next layer the chocolate ice cream. Set in freezer.

Beat egg whites with cream of tartar until soft peaks form. Add sugar and vanilla, beating until stiff. Cover the ice cream with meringue and put under broiler for about one minute until it is golden. Serve immediately or return to freezer until serving time and top with chocolate sauce.

continued

Chocolate Sauce

2	(1-ounce) squares sweet baking chocolate
2	(1-ounce) squares unsweetened chocolate
½	cup whipping cream
½	cup sugar

Melt chocolates, sugar and half the cream in top of a double boiler. Slowly add the rest of the cream, cooking over medium heat until it begins to thicken and is the right consistency to pour. Spoon over wedges of pie.

Peppermint Frangos

"Terrific little chocolate mint pies that are superb with coffee at the end of a meal."

Makes 60 miniatures or
24 individual-size servings

1	cut butter
2	cups sifted powdered sugar
4	(1-ounce) squares unsweetened chocolate, melted
4	eggs
2	teaspoons vanilla
2	teaspoons peppermint flavoring
1	cup chocolate wafer crumbs

Cream butter and sugar until light and fluffy. Gradually add melted chocolate. Add eggs, one at a time, beating well after each addition. Mix in vanilla and peppermint.

Sprinkle half the crumbs in 60 small cupcake liners set in miniature muffin tins. Distribute filling evenly into cups; top with remaining crumbs.

Freeze until firm. Serve frozen or cold. This can also be made in an 8 x 8-inch pan and cut into squares or use 24 regular-size muffin tins.

Desserts

Chocolate Mousse Royale

"One of the most mouth-watering chocolate extravaganzas you can make."

Makes 15 Servings

2	cups chocolate wafer crumbs
6	tablespoons butter, melted
1	pound semi-sweet chocolate
2	eggs
4	egg yolks
2	cups whipping cream
6	tablespoons powdered sugar
4	egg whites, room temperature
2	cups whipping cream, garnish
6	tablespoons powdered sugar, garnish
	Cherry Cordials, garnish (see Candy Section)
	Chocolate curls, garnish

Combine crumbs and butter. Press into the bottom of a 9-inch springform pan. Chill for 30 minutes. Melt chocolate in the top of a double boiler; cool. Add eggs and yolks mixing well; set aside. In a mixing bowl, whip cream with powdered sugar until soft peaks form; set aside.

Beat egg whites until stiff but not dry. Gently fold egg whites and whipped cream into chocolate mixture. Pour into crust and chill at least 6 hours or preferably overnight. Whip cream and powdered sugar together; pipe on top of pie. Garnish with cherries and chocolate curls.

Marbled Mousse
Extraordinaire

*"Chocolate and white mousse swirled together and frozen
for a spectacular dessert."*

Makes 12 Servings

6	ounces sweet cooking chocolate
3	(1-ounce) squares unsweetened chocolate
10	egg yolks
1	cup sugar
½	cup Baileys Irish Cream Liqueur
1	teaspoon vanilla extract
2	cups whipping cream

Melt chocolates in top of double boiler; set aside. In large
mixing bowl, beat egg yolks; gradually add sugar until thick
and lemon colored (about 7 minutes). Add liqueur and vanilla;
mix until well blended. Take 1 cup of mixture and place in a
separate bowl; set aside. Add melted chocolate to remaining
mixture; blend together and set aside.

In a large bowl, whip cream until soft peaks form. Take 2 cups
of the whipped cream and gently fold into reserved vanilla
mixture. Fold remaining whipped cream into chocolate
mixture. Oil a 6½-cup ring mold. Fill mold by dropping ¼
cup of chocolate mixture alternately with ¼ cup of vanilla
mixture. When filled, run a knife slowly through mold several
times to produce a swirl effect.

Cover and freeze until firm about 6 hours or overnight. Before
serving, dip bottom of mold in hot water for 1 minute.
Unmold on serving plate and garnish with additional whipped
cream, chocolate shavings, cherries or strawberries.

High Spirited Mousse

*"Fragrant chocolate laced with brandy, Amaretto
and creme de cocoa."*

Makes 8 Servings

6	(1-ounce) squares unsweetened chocolate
¾	cup butter
6	eggs, separated
1	cup brown sugar, packed
2½	teaspoons cream of tartar
2½	teaspoons vanilla
1	cup whipping cream
2	tablespoons brandy
	Grated peel of 1 small orange
2	tablespoons Amaretto
2	tablespoons creme de cacao
¼	cup granulated sugar

Slowly melt chocolate and butter together in top of double boiler. Beat egg yolks and brown sugar until creamy. Gradually add chocolate mixture to egg yolk mixture, set aside.

Beat egg whites and cream of tartar until they form stiff peaks. Fold in chocolate mixture. Combine vanilla, whipping cream, brandy, orange peel, Amaretto, creme de cacao and granulated sugar. Whip until mixture forms stiff peaks. Fold into chocolate mixture.

Chill for 1 hour and pipe with a pastry tube or spoon into individual serving dishes. Chill several hours.

Chocolate Mousse Pronto

"Nothing this easy should taste so good!"

Makes 6 Servings

4	eggs, separated
¼	cup sugar
6	ounces (1 cup) semi-sweet chocolate chips
5	tablespoons boiling coffee
1	tablespoon rum
1	teaspoon vanilla (if rum is omitted, use 2 teaspoons vanilla)

In a small bowl, beat egg whites until soft peaks form, gradually add sugar until stiff; set aside.

Place chocolate pieces in a blender and whirl to break into small pieces. Add boiling coffee and blend until smooth. Add egg yolks, rum and vanilla and blend for an additional minute.

Fold chocolate mixture into egg whites. Spoon into individual souffle dishes or champagne glasses. Chill several hours until firm. Garnish with additional whipped cream and shaved chocolate, if desired.

The Chocolate Mousse

"Just the name stirs the senses with unutterable bliss."

Makes 6 Servings

4	ounces unsweetened chocolate
4	egg whites
1	cup whipping cream
¾	cup powdered sugar
½	teaspoon vanilla or rum
	Whipped cream, garnish
	Chocolate shavings, garnish

Melt chocolate in top of double boiler. Let cool to (110°); set aside. In a mixing bowl, beat egg whites until stiff; set aside.

Beat cream until frothy; gradually add powdered sugar beating until soft peaks form. Mix in vanilla and gently fold cream mixture into egg whites. Then fold in cooled chocolate until blended.

Spoon into individual serving dishes or glasses. Refrigerate at least 2 hours and serve with whipped cream and chocolate shavings.

White Chocolate Mousse

"Ravishingly elegant."

Makes 6 Servings

8	ounces white chocolate (Toblerone), chopped
½	cup whipping cream
3	eggs, separated
½	cup plus 2 tablespoons whipping cream
2	cups whipping cream, whipped
¼	teaspoon vanilla
	Tia Maria Chocolate Sauce (See Index)
	Pureed raspberries or strawberries

Melt white chocolate and ½ cup whipping cream in top of double boiler; pour into a mixing bowl. In top of double boiler, mix egg yolks and ½ cup plus 2 tablespoons whipping cream. Cook, stirring constantly, until mixture thickens enough to coat a spoon. Stir yolk mixture into melted white chocolate; cool to room temperature.

Beat egg whites until stiff; fold into chocolate mixture. Beat 2 cups whipping cream until stiff peaks form. Mix in vanilla and fold into chocolate mixture. Refrigerate at least 4 hours. To serve, pour a pool of Chocolate Sauce in individual serving dishes. Pipe or spoon mousse on top and cover with pureed raspberries or strawberries.

Chocolate Mousse Crêpes

"Frozen chocolate crepes filled with Chocolate Mousse and covered with warm Cream Anglaise Sauce. You could become a legend with this recipe alone!"

Makes 6 Servings

Mousse

1	(6 ounce) package semi-sweet chocolate chips
1½	teaspoons vanilla
	Dash of salt
1½	cups whipping cream
6	egg yolks

Combine chocolate chips, vanilla and salt in a food processor and mix 30 seconds with steel blade. Heat cream to boiling, and with processor going, add cream to chocolate.

Add egg yolks and process until smooth (about ten seconds). Let the mixture cool in the refrigerator until thickened.

Crêpes

1	cup milk
½	cup flour
¼	cup sugar
2	eggs

continued

2	tablespoons unsweetened cocoa powder
1	tablespoon butter, melted
1	teaspoon vanilla
	Melted butter

Combine milk, flour, sugar, eggs, cocoa, 1 tablespoon butter and vanilla in a blender (do not use a food processor). Mix on low until combined; do not overblend. Allow batter to stand covered at least 1 hour.

Brush a 6 to 8-inch crepe pan with melted butter and place over medium heat. When butter sizzles, pour about ¼ cup of crepe batter in pan; swirl and pour excess back into blender jar. Cook until bottom darkens slightly and edges look dry. Be careful—cocoa burns easily. If desired, cook on reverse side approximately one minute.

Turn out onto damp paper toweling and repeat until all the batter is used. Grease the crepe pan as needed. Keep finished crepes covered with damp paper toweling.

Put 1 heaping tablespoon of mousse on each finished crepe; roll up cigarette fashion. Place on baking sheet and freeze. When frozen, place in plastic bags and keep in the freezer until 10 minutes before serving time. Serve with warm Crème Anglaise Sauce.

continued

Crème Anglaise Sauce

4	egg yolks
½	cup sugar
1½	cups half and half cream
1	tablespoon vanilla

Beat egg yolks and sugar together until pale yellow and thick. Heat cream to boiling point; slowly pour into the yolk mixture, beating constantly.

Transfer to a saucepan and cook over low heat, stirring constantly until mixture thickens and coats a spoon (about 20 minutes). Remove from heat, beat a minute and add vanilla. To serve, place 2 crepes on a dessert plate and spoon warm sauce over top.

Hot Chocolate Soufflé

"Serve it right from the oven with whipped cream and grated chocolate or Creme Anglaise Sauce."

Makes 6 Servings

6	ounces sweet baking chocolate
½	cup plus 1 teaspoon sugar
⅓	cup milk
4	egg yolks, beaten
6	egg whites
¼	cup sugar

Butter 6 (½-cup) souffle dishes or 1 (3-cup) souffle dish. Sprinkle buttered dish with sugar, shaking out excess. In a saucepan, combine chocolate, ½ cup plus 1 teaspoon sugar and milk. Cook and stir over low heat until chocolate melts. Let cool slightly, beat in egg yolks; set aside.

In mixing bowl, beat egg whites until firm; gradually add ¼ cup sugar until stiff. Stir in half of whites into chocolate mixture; gently fold in remaining whites until blended. Gently spoon into prepared dishes. Bake at 350° for 20 minutes. Serve with additional whipped cream or Crème Anglaise Sauce.

continued

Crème Anglaise Sauce

1   cup whipping cream
2   eggs, beaten
1   teaspoon vanilla or Creme de Cocoa
1   tablespoon sugar

Mix cream, eggs, vanilla and sugar in top of double boiler. Whisk until well blended.

Cook, stirring frequently, over simmering water until thickened; cool. Pass sauce (at room temperature or chilled) separately to spoon over souffle.

Chilled Chocolate Soufflé

"A grand dessert for your next dinner party."

Makes 10 Servings

2	envelopes unflavored gelatin
2	cups milk
1	cup sugar
¼	teaspoon salt
4	eggs, separated
12	ounces semi-sweet chocolate chips
1	teaspoon vanilla
2	cups heavy cream, whipped
	Sweetened whipped cream, garnish
	Chocolate curls, garnish

Combine gelatin and milk in saucepan; let sit 5 minutes to soften gelatin. In a small bowl, combine ½ cup of the sugar, salt and egg yolks; blend until smooth; pour into saucepan. Add chocolate and cook over low heat; stirring constantly, until gelatin is dissolved and chocolate is melted (about 8 minutes). Remove from heat and beat with rotary beater or whisk until smooth. Stir in vanilla and refrigerate until mixture mounds slightly when dropped from spoon.

Beat egg whites until soft peaks form; gradually add remaining ½ cup sugar until stiff. Fold into chocolate mixture. Then fold in whipped cream. Turn into a 1½-quart souffle dish with 3-inch wide aluminum foil collar. Refrigerate 2 hours or until set. Remove collar and decorate with whipped cream and chocolate curls.

Chocolate Lush

"An easy, four layer dessert that's always a hit at the family gathering."

Makes 12 Servings

Crust

1	cup flour
½	cup butter or margarine
1	cup chopped pecans

Mix together and press into a 9 x 13-inch pan. Bake at 350° for 25 minutes; cool.

Cream Cheese Layer

8	ounces cream cheese
1	cup powdered sugar
1	(12–ounce) container frozen whipped topping, thawed

Mix cream cheese and powdered sugar together. Fold in whipped topping and spread over crust.

continued

Chocolate Layer

2   (4-ounce) packages chocolate fudge instant
           pudding
3   cups milk

Mix pudding with milk. Let set and spread over cream cheese layer.

Topping

1   (12-ounce) container frozen whipped
           topping, thawed
       Shaved chocolate, garnish

Spread whipped topping over chocolate layer; sprinkle with shaved chocolate. Refrigerate at least 2 hours or, even better, overnight.

Classic Chocolate Fondue

"Let your guests indulge with this instant party hit."

9	ounces Swiss chocolate (Toblerone)
½	cup whipping cream
2	tablespoons Kirsch, Cognac or Cointreau
*	Assorted Fondue Dippers

Melt chocolate in top of double boiler. Stir in cream and Kirsch. Keep warm in chafing dish and serve with dippers.

  * Fondue Dippers: Strawberries, pineapple, bananas, marshmallows, pieces of pound cake or any favorite dipper.

White Chocolate Fondue

Substitute 9 ounces good quality white chocolate for the Swiss chocolate in the recipe above. Follow the rest of the recipe as directed.

Chocolate–Caramel Fondue

Melt 9-ounces Swiss chocolate in top of double boiler. Stir in one 12-ounce jar caramel topping. Add cream, a tablespoon at a time, until desired consistency.

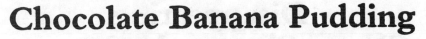

Chocolate Banana Pudding

"Brian likes this so much, he says it makes only one serving."

Makes 6 Servings

2	eggs, separated
3	cups milk
2/3	cup cocoa
1/3	cup flour
3/4	cup sugar
2	teaspoons vanilla
2	heaping tablespoons sugar
5	medium size bananas, sliced
	Vanilla wafers (about 35)

Beat egg yolks and combine with milk in saucepan. Mix in cocoa, flour and 3/4 cup sugar. Heat, stirring constantly, until mixture boils. Reduce heat and cook about 10 minutes until thick; stir in vanilla.

Layer half of the bananas on the bottom of an 8 x 8-inch cake pan. Cover with half of the vanilla wafers. Top with another layer of bananas and wafers. Pour pudding over top; press down with spoon when necessary, to let pudding through.

Beat egg whites until they softly mound; gradually add 2 tablespoons sugar until it dissolves. Spread mixture on top of pudding. Bake at 350° until lightly browned. Serve either warm or cold.

Disappearing
Choco-Cheesecake Squares

"A delicious dessert that's microwave ready in only 15 minutes."

1¼	cups chocolate wafer crumbs
1	tablespoon sugar
3	tablespoons melted butter
2	(8-ounce) packages cream cheese, room temperature
2	(1-ounce) squares unsweetened chocolate, melted
¾	cup sugar
¼	cup flour
3	eggs
1	tablespoon vanilla
½	cup chopped pecans
	Strawberries, garnish (optional)

Mix crumbs, sugar and butter together; press into bottom of an 8-inch square glass dish. Microwave on high for 2 minutes, turning a half turn after 1 minute; set aside and let cool.

In a mixing bowl, beat cream cheese until fluffy. Add chocolate, sugar, flour, eggs and vanilla, mixing well. Pour into crumb crust and sprinkle pecans over top.

Microwave 12 to 15 minutes on low or defrost, turning a quarter turn every 4 minutes. Cheesecake is done when center is set. Chill several hours and garnish with fresh strawberries, if desired.

Cream Puff Ring with Chocolate Mousse Filling

"Light and luscious."

Makes 10 Servings

Cream Puff Ring

1	cup water
½	cup butter
1	teaspoon sugar
¼	teaspoon salt
1	cup flour
4	large eggs

Combine water, butter, sugar and salt in a saucepan; bring to boil. Add flour all at once and beat with wooden spoon until it leaves the sides of pan. Remove from heat and beat 2 minutes; cool.

Add eggs, one at a time, beating well after each addition. Place mounds of dough in a wreath shape on a well greased baking sheet.

Bake at 400° for 40 minutes. Let cool and slice lengthwise. Place bottom slice on a serving plate. Fill with Chocolate Mousse. Place top slice over mousse and frost with Chocolate Glaze.

continued

Chocolate Mousse Filling

1   cup butter, softened
1   cup sugar
4   (1-ounce) squares unsweetened chocolate,
         melted
2   teaspoons vanilla
6   eggs

Cream butter and sugar until light and fluffy. Beat in chocolate and vanilla. Add eggs, one at a time, beating well (about 2 minutes) between each addition. Continue beating until sugar dissolves. Chill at least 2 hours before filling cream puff.

Chocolate Glaze

2   (1-ounce) squares semi-sweet chocolate
2   tablespoons butter
       Toasted slivered almonds, garnish

Melt chocolate and butter; stir until smooth. Pour over cream puff ring and sprinkle with toasted almonds.

World Class Chocolate Cups

"An impressive grand finale."

Makes 8 Servings

6   ounces semi-sweet or sweet cooking
         chocolate
2   tablespoons butter

Melt chocolate and butter in top of double boiler. Place 8 foil or paper baking cups in a muffin pan. Spread chocolate on bottom and sides of cups with a teaspoon or pastry brush.

Refrigerate for about 10 minues and apply a second coating if necessary. Refrigerate until set. Carefully peel off paper or foil; refrigerate or freeze until ready to use. Fill with any flavor ice cream or chocolate mousse.

Pots de Crème au Chocolat

*"From one of the chocolate capitals of the world . . .
a French custard with a marvelous texture and flavor."*

Makes 6 Servings

8	ounces semi-sweet chocolate
1½	cups half and half cream
½	cup whipping cream
	Dash of salt
5	egg yolks, well beaten
1	tablespoon rum or brandy
	Whipped cream, garnish
	Chocolate shavings, garnish

Combine chocolate, creams and salt in double boiler. Cook over low heat, stirring constantly, until chocolate is melted and cream is scalded. Mix in yolks and rum.

Pour into 6 demi-tasse, individual souffle, custard cups or petits pots. Chill at least 2 hours. Serve with a dollop of whipped cream topped with shaved chocolate.

Dark Fudge Ice Cream

"Purely decadent — A chocoholic's dream come true!"

Makes 1½ Quarts

6	(1–ounce) squares unsweetened chocolate
2	tablespoons butter
2	cups sugar
⅓	cup light corn syrup
2	cups half and half cream
4	eggs
2	teaspoons vanilla extract
2	cups whipping cream

In a large, heavy saucepan, melt chocolate and butter over low heat, stirring often. Stir in sugar, corn syrup and ⅔ cup of the half and half. Stir over medium-low heat until mixture comes to a boil. Simmer 4 minutes without stirring; set aside.

In a small bowl, beat eggs until blended. Stir in ½ cup of hot chocolate mixture. Stir egg mixture into remaining chocolate mixture. Cook and stir over medium heat until slightly thickened, about 1 minute.

Cool to lukewarm. Stir in vanilla, whipping cream and the rest of the half and half. Freeze in ice-cream maker according to manufacturer's directions.

Irish Cream Chocolate Chip Ice Cream

"Fabulously rich and smooth with that incredible Irish Cream flavor. You don't even need an ice-cream freezer."

Makes ½ Gallon

2½	cups whipping cream
3	large eggs, separated
¾	cup sugar
1	teaspoon vanilla
¼	cup Bailey's Irish Cream
4	ounces semi-sweet chocolate, melted and kept warm

In a large bowl, whip 2 cups of the whipping cream until soft peaks form. Refrigerate.

In a double boiler, combine the egg yolks, sugar, vanilla and the remaining ½ cup whipping cream. Whisk until the mixture is hot and the sugar has dissolved, about 8 to 10 minutes.

Refrigerate several hours or place in freezer until mixture is very cold and thick (stir several times). Stir in Bailey's Irish Cream. Add the warm melted chocolate (chocolate will clump).

Beat egg whites until stiff. Fold egg whites and refrigerated whipped cream into chocolate mixture. Pour into a 2-quart pan or dish. Freeze 8 hours until firm. Remove from freezer 5 to 10 minutes before serving.

Chocolate Sorbet

"Entices the taste buds the moment it touches the tongue."

Makes 1 Quart

4	(1-ounce) squares unsweetened chocolate
1	quart water
1½	cups sugar
	Chocolate leaves, garnish

With a knife, food processor or blender, chop the chocolate into very small pieces; set aside.

In a heavy saucepan, heat water and sugar together. Add chocolate and simmer for 20 to 30 minutes, stirring occasionally until mixture is smooth and not grainy.

Cool thoroughly and pour into ice-cream maker. Freeze according to manufacturer's directions. Serve in a champagne glass with a chocolate leaf for garnish.

Chocolate was described in a 1916 cookbook as follows:

"It is a perfect food, as wholesome as delicious, a beneficent restorer of exhausted power; but its quality must be good and it must be carefully prepared."

From Chocolate and Cocoa Recipes
By Miss Parloa

Miss Parloa's Chocolate Ice Cream

"A real old-fashioned recipe."

3	cups milk
3	tablespoons flour
2	cups sugar
2	eggs, slightly beaten
¼	teaspoon salt
2½	ounces unsweetened chocolate
2	tablespoons hot water
1	quart cream

Scald milk. Mix flour and one-half the sugar and add eggs and salt. Add gradually to scalded milk, stirring constantly until mixture thickens, and afterwards occasionally, cooking twenty minutes.

Melt chocolate, add one-fourth cup of the reserved sugar, and hot water. Stir until smooth, and add to cooked mixture. Strain, and add remaining sugar and cream. Cool and freeze in an ice-cream freezer, using three parts finely crushed ice to one part rock salt.

White Chocolate Ice Cream

"You'll be enthralled by the smooth texture and incredible richness of a truly great ice cream."

½	pound good quality white chocolate
2	tablespoons butter
1	cup milk
5	egg yolks
¼	cup sugar
1	tablespoon light corn syrup
2	cups whipping cream

Cut white chocolate into small pieces. In a heavy (2-quart) saucepan, combine chocolate, butter and milk. Stir constantly over low heat until chocolate and butter melt; remove from heat.

In a mixing bowl, beat egg yolks and sugar for 5 minutes until thick. Stir into chocolate mixture with corn syrup. Cook, stirring constantly, over low heat for 8 to 10 minutes until thick and mixture coats back of metal spoon. Remove from heat.

Stir in cream and let sit until room temperature. Freeze in ice-cream maker according to manufacturer's directions.

French Chocolate Ice Cream

"Smooth and wonderful—you don't even need an ice cream freezer."

Makes 1 Quart

3	egg yolks
⅓	cup water
¼	cup sugar
6	ounces semi-sweet chocolate, chopped
1½	cups whipping cream, softly whipped

In a mixing bowl, beat yolks until lemon colored; set aside. In a saucepan, heat water and sugar; stir over high heat until sugar dissolves and mixture comes to boil. Boil without stirring for 3 minutes. Add chocolate; remove from heat; stir until chocolate melts.

Gradually (beating slowly) add hot chocolate mixture to yolks; beat until smooth. With wooden spoon, stir occasionally until cooled to room temperature. With rubber spatula, gently fold in whipped cream until thoroughly blended. Pour into an 8-inch loaf pan. Cover with aluminum foil and freeze until firm.

Incredibly Easy
Rocky Road Ice Cream

*"A scooper dooper treat for the kids.
It tastes like pudding and ice cream."*

Makes 2½ Quarts

1	(14-ounce) can sweetened condensed milk
1½	cups (16-ounce can) chocolate flavored syrup
1	cup miniature marshmallows
½	cup chopped walnuts, pecans or peanuts
½	cup semi-sweet chocolate mini-chips

In a large mixing bowl, stir milk and syrup together until blended. Add marshmallows, nuts and chips.

Whip cream until soft peaks form. Fold into chocolate mixture until well blended. Pour into a 2½-quart freezer container. Freeze 6 hours or until firm.

Hot Fudge Ice Cream Bars

"This luscious dessert is great to keep on hand in the freezer."

Makes 16 Servings

42	cream filled chocolate cookies, crushed (Oreos)
½	cup butter or margarine, melted
½	gallon vanilla ice cream, softened
1½	cups Spanish peanuts or mixed nuts
½	cup sugar
1½	cups evaporated milk
⅓	cup butter or margarine
⅔	cup semi-sweet chocolate chips

Combine crushed cookies with ½ cup butter. Pat in a 9 x 13-inch glass baking dish; freeze. Spread ice cream over crumbs; sprinkle with half the nuts; freeze.

In a saucepan bring sugar, evaporated milk, ⅓ cup butter and chocolate chips to a boil. Cook until fairly thick; cool and spread over ice cream. Top with remaining peanuts; freeze.

Remove from freezer 5 to 10 minutes before serving and cut into 2½-inch bars. Will keep in freezer for several weeks.

Chocolate and Cream Revel Bars

"An irresistible frozen dessert with a peanut butter crust and marbled chocolate and cream filling."

Makes 16 Servings

Crust

½	cup brown sugar
½	cup peanut butter
¼	cup butter or margarine, softened
1	cup flour

In a mixing bowl, cream brown sugar, peanut butter and butter until light and fluffy. Add flour and blend until crumbly. Pat ⅔ of mixture (reserve rest for topping) into an ungreased 9 x 13-inch pan. Bake at 350° for 8 to 10 minutes until golden brown; cool.

Filling

8	ounces cream cheese, softened
½	cup sugar
¼	cup peanut butter
1	teaspoon vanilla
2	eggs

continued

1   cup whipping cream, whipped
6   ounces (1 cup) semi-sweet chocolate chips

In a mixing bowl, beat cream cheese, sugar, peanut butter and vanilla until smooth and creamy. Add eggs, one at a time, beating well after each addition. Fold in whipped cream and pour over cooled crust.

Melt chocolate and drizzle over filling. With a knife gently cut through to marble. Sprinkle with reserved crumbs. Freeze several hours or overnight. Remove from freezer 10 minutes before serving.

Chocolate Frosted
Ice Cream Roll

"Impressive, festive and it can be made well ahead of time."

Makes 8 Servings

½	cup flour
½	cup cocoa
1	teaspoon baking powder
¼	teaspoon salt
4	eggs, separated
¾	cup sugar
½	teaspoon vanilla extract
¼	teaspoon almond extract
1	quart vanilla ice cream, softened (any flavor ice cream will do)
	Chocolate frosting
	Chopped pistachio nuts, garnish
	Maraschino cherries, garnish

Sift flour, cocoa, baking powder and salt together; set aside. Beat egg whites (at room temperature) until foamy; gradually add sugar and continue beating until stiff; set aside. Beat egg yolks until thick and lemon colored; stir in extracts. Fold into egg white mixture. Gently fold in flour mixture. Spread in a greased and waxed paper-lined 15 x 10 x 1-inch jellyroll pan (after lining pan with waxed paper, grease paper). Bake at 350° for 12 minutes.

continued

Remove cake from oven and immediately turn out onto damp cloth. Peel off waxed paper. Starting at wide end, roll up cake and towel together. Cool on wire rack, seam-side down for 30 minutes. Unroll cake; remove towel. Spread ice cream evenly over cake. Gently roll cake back up. Place on large baking sheet and freeze until ice cream is firm.

Frost cake with chocolate frosting; freeze until serving time. Garnish with pistachios and cherries.

Chocolate Frosting

¼	cup butter or margarine, softened
3	tablespoons milk
3	tablespoons unsweetened cocoa powder
2	cups sifted powdered sugar
1	teaspoon vanilla extract

Combine all ingredients and beat until smooth.

Chocolate Meringue Torte

"A superior dessert with chocolate cream nestled between three layers of meringue and topped off with chocolate curls."

(Special thanks to my sister, Karen Rubin, for this recipe.)

Makes 8 Servings

Meringue

3   egg whites
1   cup less 1 tablespoon superfine sugar

Grease and flour 2 cookie sheets. Use an 8-inch round cake pan and place it on cookie sheet. Run your finger around pan, so it forms a circle in the flour; remove pan. Make 2 more circles (this will be your guide to form 3 circular meringues).

Beat 3 egg whites until soft peaks form, gradually add sugar, beating until stiff peaks form. Spoon evenly into prepared circles. Bake at 300° for 30 minutes until layers are firm and golden brown.

Chocolate Cream

⅔   cup heavy cream
7   ounces semi-sweet chocolate
3½   ounces unsweetened chocolate

continued

4	tablespoons butter
4	egg whites
1	cup less 1 tablespoon superfine sugar
	Chocolate curls, garnish
	Powdered sugar, garnish

In top of double boiler, heat cream and chocolates, stirring until chocolate melts. Add butter and stir until melted; set aside. Beat egg whites until soft peaks form. Gradually add sugar, beating until stiff peaks form; set aside.

Fill bottom of double boiler with water and ice. Set chocolate mixture in water; with hand mixer, beat at high speed until light and fluffy. Fold chocolate into beaten egg whites until thoroughly mixed.

Place 1 meringue layer on serving plate. Cover with ⅓ of Chocolate Cream. Repeat with 2nd and 3rd layer. Garnish with chocolate curls. Chill several hours before serving. Sprinkle with powdered sugar and cut into pieces with sharp serrated knife.

Double Chocolate Eclairs

"The oohs and aahs make it worth all the effort."

Makes 14 Eclairs

½   cup butter or margarine
1   cup boiling water
1   cup all-purpose flour
¼   teaspoon salt
4   eggs, beaten
       Chocolate Custard Filling
       Chocolate Glaze

In a saucepan, heat butter and water to full rolling boil. Reduce heat and add flour and salt all at once, mixing vigorously with wooden spoon until mixture forms a ball. Add eggs in 6 additions, beating after each addition until smooth. (An electric mixer at low speed works well).

Pipe dough through a pastry tube, making 1 x 4-inch strips, on a greased baking sheet. Bake at 400° for 40 to 45 minutes. Remove to wire racks to cool; cut in half and remove soft centers. Just before serving, fill bottoms with Chocolate Custard Filling and replace tops. Frost with Chocolate Glaze. Store in refrigerator.

Chocolate Custard Filling

3   cups milk
2   (1-ounce) squares unsweetened chocolate,
         chopped

continued

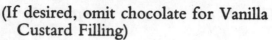

> (If desired, omit chocolate for Vanilla
> Custard Filling)

¾	cup sugar
6	tablespoons cornstarch
½	teaspoon salt
3	eggs, beaten
1	tablespoon butter
2	teaspoons vanilla extract

Scald milk in top part of double boiler over boiling water. Add chocolate and stir until blended. Mix sugar, cornstarch and salt together; gradually stir it into milk mixture. Continue to cook, stirring until thick. Cover; cook for 10 minutes longer, stirring occasionally.

Add small amount of mixture to eggs; return to double boiler and cook for 5 minutes; add butter. Put in bowl and sprinkle small amount of sugar over top to prevent skin from forming. Chill; stir in vanilla.

Chocolate Glaze

1	(1-ounce) square unsweetened chocolate
1	tablespoon butter
1	cup sifted powdered sugar
2 to 3	tablespoons milk

In a saucepan, melt chocolate and butter together over low heat. Stir in powdered sugar and milk, blending until smooth and creamy.

Candies
&
Toppings

Chocolate-Covered Cherries

"Indulge your chocolate craving with only the best."

Makes about 50

1	(16-ounce) jar plus 1 (10-ounce) jar mara- schino cherries with stems (need about 50)
3	tablespoons butter, softened
3	tablespoons light corn syrup
¼	teaspoon salt
2	cups sifted powdered sugar
12	ounces semi-sweet chocolate chips
4	(1-ounce) squares unsweetened chocolate
1	tablespoon solid vegetable shortening

Drain cherries well; pat very dry with paper towels. Mix butter, syrup and salt until well blended; gradually add powdered sugar.

Knead in bowl until smooth and stiff enough to shape around cherry. With greased hands, shape ½ teaspoon sugar mixture around each cherry. Place on waxed paper-lined baking sheet. Chill 2 hours or until firm.

Melt chocolates and shortening in double boiler. Hold cherry by stem and dip in chocolate. Place on waxed paper-lined baking sheet. Chill until firm. Store in airtight container in refrigerator.

Cherry Cordials

"Great by themselves or use to decorate a pie or cake to the nth degree with whipped cream, chocolate shavings and Cherry Cordials."

13   large maraschino cherries with stems
½   cup brandy or Chambord liqueur
5   ounces semi-sweet chocolate, melted

Drain cherries well. Soak cherries in brandy for several hours. Place cherries in freezer until just frozen. Dry with paper towels and dip each by stem into chocolate, swirling until covered. Place on wax paper-lined cookie sheets. Chill in refrigerator until ready to use.

Chocolate Candy Cookie Brittle

*"A thin butter cookie layer, blanketed by thick chocolate—
it's addictive!"*

Makes 3 Dozen Pieces

½   cup butter, softened
½   cup brown sugar
1   egg yolk
1   cup flour
½   teaspoon vanilla
1   (8-ounce) milk chocolate bar
½   (8-ounce) dark chocolate bar
1   (4-ounce) German's sweet chocolate bar
1   cup chopped pecans

Cream butter and sugar until fluffy. Add egg yolk, flour and vanilla, mixing well. Spread on ungreased jelly roll pan approximately ¼-inch thick. Bake at 350° for 15 minutes.

Melt chocolates in top of double boiler. While cookie is still warm, spread on chocolate. Sprinkle with pecans. Place in freezer until frozen. Remove and break into pieces with point of knife. Best served shortly after removing from freezer.

Chocolate Truffles

"One of the most luxurious forms of chocolate."

Makes 2½ Dozen

½	pound semi-sweet chocolate (Swiss or French is best)
⅓	cup heavy cream
⅓	cup unsalted butter
2	large egg yolks
	Unsweetened cocoa

Melt chocolate with cream in a double boiler, stirring until smooth. Add butter and stir until creamy. Blend in egg yolks. Chill until firm.

Take a teaspoonful of mixture and roll into a ball. Then roll in cocoa. Place in paper bonbon cups. Chill or freeze.

Chocolate is a native to the North American Hemisphere. The Spanish invaders, under Cortez, brought the new treasure back to Spain. Slowly the German and French learned about the secret of chocolate and it spread throughout Europe.

Spirited Deep Dark Truffles

"Promise me anything . . . but give me Deep Dark Truffles!"

Makes 3½ Dozen

Truffles

4	(1–ounce) squares unsweetened chocolate
6	tablespoons unsalted butter, cut into bits
¼	cup plus 2 tablespoons sugar
1	cup unsweetened cocoa powder, (preferably Dutch process)
½	cup heavy cream, warmed
½	cup rum, brandy or flavored liqueur
4	egg yolks

In a medium saucepan, over low heat, melt the chocolate. Add the butter and stir until melted. Stir in the sugar, cocoa, warm cream, rum and egg yolks. Whisk until the mixture is smooth and very creamy, about 5 minutes.

Pour the truffle mixture into an 8 x 8-inch baking pan. Chill or freeze about 2 hours, until firm enough to handle.

Take 2 to 3 teaspoonfuls of mixture and roll into 1-inch balls with your hands. Place on waxed paper-lined baking sheet. Chill or freeze until firm.

continued

Truffle Coating

12   ounces semi-sweet chocolate, coarsely
            chopped

Melt chocolate in top of doubler boiler. Use a dipping fork or regular fork and dip truffles until thinly coated with chocolate. Let set on lined baking sheet until hardened. Store in refrigerator.

Chocolate Caramels

"Creamy, dreamy, thick and chewy."

Makes 5 Dozen

2	cups sugar
1½	cups corn syrup
2	cups whipping cream
1	cup butter
4	(1–ounce) squares unsweetened chocolate
1½	cups walnuts or pecans (optional)
2	teaspoons vanilla

In a heavy saucepan bring sugar, syrup, 1 cup cream and butter to a rolling boil. Gradually add second cup of cream, making sure boil is not disturbed. Cook until mixture reaches hard ball stage (260°). Remove from heat and stir in chocolate until it melts. Add nuts and vanilla.

Pour into a greased 8-inch square pan. Cool and cut into squares. Wrap each square individually in waxed paper.

Classic Fudge

"The kind you dream about!"

Makes 5 Dozen Squares

4	cups sugar
4	ounces unsweetened cocoa (preferably Dutch process)
4	cups whipping cream
1	tablespoon white corn syrup
	Dash of salt
1½	teaspoons vanilla
2	tablespoons butter

Sift sugar and cocoa together. Place in a large heavy pan with the cream. Stir constantly over medium-high heat until sugar is dissolved (be sure to wipe sides of pan free of sugar crystals). When mixture comes to a boil, add corn syrup. Let mixture boil (do not stir) over medium heat until firm ball stage (242°F).

Pour mixture into a large bowl and add salt, vanilla and butter. Do not stir. Let cool undisturbed for ½ hour or until lukewarm (110°F). With electric mixer, beat until thick and loses gloss. Pour into a greased 9 x 13-inch pan. Let stand until firm (could be several hours).

Fudge Cups

"Chocolate fans—it's a chocolate cookie crust filled with fudge!"

Makes 4 Dozen

1	cup sugar
½	cup butter or margarine, softened
1	egg
2	(1-ounce) squares unsweetened chocolate, melted
¼	teaspoon salt
½	teaspoon vanilla
1¾	cups flour, sifted

In a mixing bowl, cream sugar and butter until light and fluffy. Mix in egg, chocolate, salt and vanilla; gradually add flour until well mixed. Shape dough into 1-inch balls. Press balls in bottom and sides of greased miniature muffin cups (can also line with paper baking cups). Bake at 350° for 8 to 10 minutes. Cool for 5 to 10 minutes; remove from pans. When cool, fill with Fudge Filling.

Fudge Filling

1½	cups sugar
1½	ounces (1½ squares) unsweetened chocolate, cut in pieces
⅓	cup milk

continued

¼	cup butter or margarine
3	tablespoons corn syrup
⅛	teaspoon salt
1	teaspoon vanilla
	Pecans, chopped fine, garnish (optional)

In a saucepan cook all ingredients, except nuts, over low heat until chocolate is melted, stirring occasionally. Bring mixture to boil and boil for 1 minute. Remove from heat; stir in vanilla. Beat to cool slightly; spoon into prepared cups. Sprinkle with chopped nuts. Chill until firm.

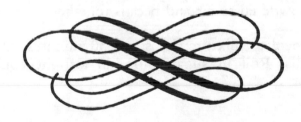

Chocolate Bourbon Balls

"A special spirited holiday treat."

Makes 5 Dozen

6	ounces semi-sweet chocolate chips
½	cup bourbon
3	tablespoons light corn syrup
2½	cups vanilla wafer crumbs
½	cup sifted powdered sugar
1	cup finely chopped pecans
	Sugar

Melt chocolate in top of double boiler. Remove from heat and stir in bourbon and corn syrup; set aside. In a large bowl, mix crumbs, powdered sugar and pecans together.

Stir in chocolate mixture; let stand 30 minutes. Shape into 1-inch balls. Roll in sugar. Store in airtight container in refrigerator.

Nut Goodies

"Tastes just like the candy bar—chocolate, a maple cream layer and more chocolate."

Makes 30 Squares

6	ounces semi-sweet chocolate chips
6	ounces butterscotch chips
1	cup peanut butter
½	cup butter or margarine
2	tablespoons vanilla pudding mix
¼	cup evaporated milk
½ to 1	teaspoon maple flavoring
1¾ to 2	cups sifted powdered sugar
6	ounces peanuts or mixed nuts

Melt chips and peanut butter in top of double boiler until mixture is melted and creamy. Pour half of mixture in a greased 8 x 8-inch pan.

In a separate pan, boil butter, pudding mix and evaporated milk for one minute. Add maple flavoring and powdered sugar and stir until creamy. Pour over chocolate layer in pan.

Top with remaining chocolate. Sprinkle nuts on top. Refrigerate and cut into 1-inch squares.

Chocolate Mocha

"A subtle brandy flavor makes this candy especially good."

Makes 60 Balls

12	ounces semi-sweet chocolate chips
4	egg yolks
1½	cups powdered sugar
1	cup soft butter
3	teaspoons instant coffee powder
4	tablespoons brandy or rum
2	teaspoons vanilla
1	cup finely chopped pecans

Melt chocolate in a double boiler and set aside. In a mixing bowl, beat egg yolks until lemon colored. Gradually add sugar and butter until smooth. Dissolve coffee in brandy and add to egg mixture. Blend in melted chocolate and vanilla; mix thoroughly.

Chill until hardened; shape into small balls and roll in chopped pecans. Store in refrigerator and serve chilled.

Rocky Road Candy

"Absolutely addictive!"

Makes 4 Dozen Squares

1   (12-ounce) package semi-sweet chocolate
        chips
2   (1-ounce) squares unsweetened chocolate
1   (14-ounce) can sweetened condensed milk
2   tablespoons butter
2   cups whole toasted walnuts or peanuts
1   (10 ½-ounce) package miniature
        marshmallows

Melt chocolates, milk and butter in a double boiler; cook and stir until creamy. Remove from heat and stir in nuts and marshmallows. Pour mixture into a waxed paper-lined 13 x 9-inch pan. Cut into 1½-inch squares. Store in refrigerator.

*The annual Potter Family Reunion was the scene
for a chocolate cook-off. Top honors and a blue ribbon
went to Paige Potter for this delectable confection.*

Peanut Butter Bon Bons

*"Peanut Butter Cup fans—watch out! These are even better and so
simple to make."*

Makes about 65

4	cups crunchy peanut butter
1	pound powdered sugar
1	(12-ounce) box Rice Crispies (lightly crushed)
½	cup butter, melted

Mix all ingredients together until well blended. With hands,
roll into 1-inch balls. Dip each ball into chocolate coating and
place on waxed paper until cool. Store in refrigerator.

Chocolate Coating

1	(12-ounce) package semi-sweet chocolate chips
2	(8-ounce) milk chocolate candy bars
½	bar paraffin
1	teaspoon vanilla

Melt all ingredients in top of a double boiler. Stir until smooth.

Easy Million Dollar Fudge

"Mamie Eisenhower made this fudge for Dwight while they were still courting. He coined the name because it tasted like a million!"

Makes about 5 Pounds

4½	cups sugar
	Pinch salt
2	tablespoons butter
1	(13-ounce) can evaporated milk
12	ounces semi-sweet chocolate
12	ounces German's sweet chocolate
2	cups marshmallow cream
2	cups chopped pecans or walnuts

In a large heavy saucepan, combine sugar, salt, butter and milk. Bring to boil and boil for 6 minutes, stirring constantly. Put chocolates in a large bowl, and pour boiling syrup over; beat until melted. Stir in marshmallow cream and nuts.

Pour into a buttered 9 x 13-inch pan. Let cool until firm and cut into squares. Store in tightly covered container. Refrigerate if kitchen is too warm.

Coconut Creams

"Great for gifts at holiday time."

Makes 6 Dozen

⅔	cup sweetened condensed milk
1	pound powdered sugar
½	cup butter, softened
1	cup flaked coconut
1	cup finely chopped walnuts or pecans
16	ounces semi-sweet chocolate chips

Mix milk, powdered sugar and butter together until well blended and creamy. Stir in coconut and walnuts until well mixed; chill for 1 hour. Form into 1-inch balls; chill for 2 hours.

Melt chocolate in top of double boiler, stirring constantly. Remove from heat; dip each bon bon in chocolate. Place on waxed paper to cool. Chill in refrigerator.

Hot-Fudge Sauce

"As decadently rich as they come."
"This sauce is perfect for your favorite chocophilic."
Chocophilic: from the Greek meaning someone who loves chocolate.

½	cup butter
2	(1-ounce) squares unsweetened chocolate
2	(1-ounce) squares semi-sweet chocolate
1	cup sugar
1	cup heavy cream
⅛	teaspoon salt
2	teaspoons vanilla

In a heavy saucepan, melt butter and chocolates over low heat. Blend in sugar, cream and salt. Stir over low heat for 5–8 minutes until thick and creamy. Remove from heat and stir in vanilla. Serve warm.

Caramel Fudge Topping

"Wonderfully thick and creamy."

Makes 10 Servings

⅓	cup whole milk
1	(16-ounce) package caramels
4	ounces semi-sweet chocolate chips
1	cup vanilla ice cream, softened
1	teaspoon vanilla

Heat milk and caramels in the top of a double boiler, stir until smooth and creamy. Add chocolate and stir until melted. Mix in ice cream and vanilla. Serve warm over ice cream.

Milky Way Fudge Topping

"Outrageous."

Makes 3 Cups

6	(2.1-ounce) Milky Way Candy Bars, cut up
6	(1-ounce) squares semi-sweet chocolate, cut up
1	cup milk
1⅓	cups chopped pecans or pecan halves (optional)

In the top of a double boiler, combine candy bars, chocolate and milk together. Cook, stirring constantly, until chocolate is melted and mixture is smooth. Stir in nuts.

Serve warm over ice cream or cool and it will thicken. Store leftovers in refrigerator and reheat over low heat.

Tia Maria Chocolate Sauce

"Smooth, silky chocolate with a fabulous flavor."

Makes 2½ Cups

½	cup unsweetened cocoa (preferably Dutch-process)
1	cup sugar
6	tablespoons cornstarch
½	cup water
½	cup light corn syrup
2	(1-ounce) squares unsweetened chocolate
½	cup butter
½	cup Tia Maria liqueur

In a large, heavy saucepan, mix cocoa, sugar and cornstarch. Add water and corn syrup and mix until smooth. Cook over medium heat until mixture boils. Add chocolate and stir until melted.

Reduce heat and cook 5 minutes more, stirring constantly. Add butter and stir until melted; remove from heat. Add Tia Maria and stir until blended. Let cool, then refrigerate.

Fabulous Cocoa Fudge Sauce

"Pour it on!"

½	cup sugar
2	tablespoons unsweetened cocoa powder
⅓	cup milk
¼	cup light corn syrup
1	(1-ounce) square unsweetened chocolate, chopped
2	tablespoons butter
⅓	cup heavy cream
1	teaspoon vanilla

In a heavy saucepan, combine sugar, cocoa, milk and corn syrup. Cook over low heat, stirring constantly until it comes to a boil; boil for 8 minutes.

Take off heat, stir in chocolate and butter until melted. Gradually add heavy cream until blended. Continue cooking and stirring over medium heat until it boils; boil 2 minutes.

Take off heat; stir in vanilla and cool. Store in tightly covered jar in refrigerator.

Dark Chocolate Sauce

"The deepest, darkest and richest of all."

Makes 1½ Cups

3	(1-ounce) squares unsweetened chocolate
1	tablespoon butter
1	cup sugar
1	(5⅓-ounce) can evaporated milk
½	teaspoon vanilla

Melt chocolate and butter together in heavy saucepan. Stir in sugar and milk. Continue cooking and stirring until sauce is thick. Stir in vanilla. Serve warm over ice cream. Store leftovers in a tightly covered jar in refrigerator.

Breads
&
Brunch

Sweet Chocolate Muffins

"How sweet it is."

Makes 18 Muffins

¼	cup butter
3	(1-ounce squares) unsweetened chocolate
2	eggs, separated
1½	cups sugar
2	cups sifted cake flour
2	teaspoons baking powder
½	teaspoon salt
1⅓	cups milk
2½	teaspoons vanilla
½	cup chopped pecans, optional
	Powdered sugar

Melt butter and chocolate in top of a double boiler; set aside. In a mixing bowl, beat egg yolks and sugar until lemon colored. Add chocolate mixture and blend well. Sift flour, baking powder and salt together. Add alternately with milk and vanilla, beating well at low speed until well blended; set aside.

Beat egg whites until stiff but not dry. Fold gently into batter with nuts. Spoon into 18 (2½-inch) muffin cups lined with paper baking cups. Bake at 375° for 20 minutes or until top springs back when touched. Cool on wire racks. Dust with powdered sugar.

Orange and Chip Muffins

"The orange and chocolate flavors make a perfect muffin for morning, noon or night."

Makes 1 dozen

1½	cups flour
½	cup sugar
2	teaspoons baking powder
½	teaspoon salt
1	egg, beaten
½	cup milk
¼	cup vegetable oil
¾	cup milk chocolate chips
2	teaspoons grated orange peel
¼	cup finely chopped pecans or walnuts

Sift flour, sugar, baking powder and salt into mixing bowl. Add the beaten egg. Mix in milk and vegetable oil, just until ingredients are mixed. Stir in chips and orange peel.

Line muffin tins with paper liners or grease tins. Fill ⅔ full with batter. Sprinkle nuts on top. Bake at 350° for 20 to 25 minutes until lightly browned.

Swiss Chocolate Almond Coffee Cake

"This may be the most perfect cake for coffee ever made."

Makes 12 Servings

2	cups sugar
4	eggs, beaten
½	cup butter, softened
4	cups sifted flour
1	tablespoon baking powder
1	teaspoon baking soda
2	cups sour cream
½	cup chocolate almond liqueur
¾	cup brown sugar
1	cup chopped pecans
½	teaspoon cinnamon
6	ounces semi-sweet chocolate, coarsely chopped

In a large mixing bowl, beat 2 cups sugar, eggs and butter until well blended. Sift together flour, baking powder and baking soda; fold into creamed mixture. Mix in sour cream and liqueur. Place half of batter in greased and floured 10-inch tube pan.

continued

In a small bowl combine brown sugar, pecans and cinnamon. Sprinkle half of mixture over batter in pan. Top with chocolate. Cover with remaining batter, then sprinkle with remaining nut mixture.

Bake at 375° for 1 hour 15 minutes or until cake tests done. Let cool for 15 minutes and remove to wire rack to finish cooling. Frost with a chocolate frosting of your choice, but it certainly is not necessary.

Chocolate Chip-Sour Cream Coffee Cake

"Only chocolate could improve this traditional favorite."

Makes 12 Servings

1	cup butter, softened
2	cups plus 4 teaspoons sugar
2	eggs
1	cup sour cream
½	teaspoon vanilla
2	cups flour
1	teaspoon baking powder
¼	teaspoon salt
¾	cup semi-sweet chocolate chips
1	cup chopped pecans
1	teaspoon cinnamon

Cream butter and 2 cups of sugar, beating until light and fluffy. Add eggs, one at a time, beating well after each addition. Add sour cream and vanilla. Mix in flour sifted with baking powder and salt.

Place ⅓ of batter in a well greased and floured bundt pan or 9-inch tube pan. Combine 4 teaspoons sugar, chocolate chips, pecans and cinnamon. Sprinkle ⅓ of sugar mixture over first layer of batter. Repeat with 2nd and 3rd layer. Bake at 350° for 50 to 60 minutes until cake tests done.

In the Chips Pumpkin Bread

"A beautiful harvest loaf, rich with pumpkin, chips, pecans, and spices."

Makes 3 Loaves

3⅓	cups flour
2	teaspoons baking soda
1	teaspoon nutmeg
3	teaspoons cinnamon
	Dash of salt
3	cups sugar
1	cup vegetable oil
⅔	cup water
1	can (16 ounces) pumpkin
4	eggs
2	cups chopped pecans or walnuts
½	cup semi-sweet chocolate chips

Mix together flour, baking soda, nutmeg, cinnamon and salt; set aside. In a mixing bowl, beat sugar and oil until well blended. Mix in dry ingredients with water, pumpkin and eggs. Stir in 1 cup of the nuts and the chips.

Pour into 3 greased and floured 8-inch loaf pans. Sprinkle remaining 1 cup of nuts over the top of the loaves. Bake at 350° for 1 hour or until done. Cool in pans before removing.

Spicy Chocolate Bread

"Has that old-fashioned, honest-to-goodness, taste appeal."

Makes 1 Loaf

⅓	cup butter or margarine, softened
2	tablespoons vegetable oil
2	eggs
2	(1-ounce) squares semi-sweet chocolate, melted
1½	cups flour
1	cup plus 1 tablespoon sugar
1	teaspoon baking soda
¼	teaspoon baking powder
½	teaspoon salt
¼	teaspoon nutmeg
½	teaspoon cinnamon
½	cup applesauce
½	cup chopped pecans or walnuts
½	cup plus 1 tablespoon mini semi-sweet chocolate chips

In a mixing bowl, combine butter, oil and eggs, mixing well. Add chocolate, flour, 1 cup of the sugar, baking soda, baking powder, salt, nutmeg, cinnamon and applesauce; mix well.

Stir in nuts and ½ cup of the chips. Pour into a greased and floured 9-inch loaf pan. Sprinkle top with remaining 1 tablespoon chocolate chips and 1 tablespoon sugar. Bake at 350° for 50 to 55 minutes. Let sit 10 minutes and remove to wire rack to cool. Cool thoroughly before slicing.

Date, Chips, and Nut Bread

"Slice it thin and make little cream cheese sandwiches."

Makes 1 Loaf

1	cup chopped dates
¾	cup boiling water
1	teaspoon baking soda
¼	cup butter, softened
¾	cup sugar
1	egg, beaten
	Pinch of salt
½	teaspoon vanilla
1½	cups flour
½	cup chopped pecans or walnuts
½	cup semi-sweet chocolate chips

Mix dates, boiling water and baking soda together; set aside until cool. In a mixing bowl, cream butter, sugar, and egg together. Add date mixture, salt, vanilla, and flour, mixing until blended. Stir in nuts and chips.

Pour into greased and floured 9-inch loaf pan. Bake at 325° for 1 hour or until tests done. Cool and remove from pan. Best made the day before serving. Keeps well in refrigerator or freezer.

Hint: This bread is perfect to make little cream cheese sandwiches. Just cut the bread into small rectangles and use softened cream cheese for the filling.

Banana Chocolate Chip Bread

"Never has banana bread tasted so good."

Makes 1 Loaf

1	cup sugar
½	cup margarine
2	eggs
3	bananas, mashed
2	cups flour
½	teaspoon baking soda
¾	cup chopped nuts
½ to 1	cup semi-sweet chocolate chips
½	cup chopped maraschino cherries, optional

Cream sugar and margarine well. Add eggs and blend together. Add bananas alternately with flour and baking soda until moistened. Stir in nuts, chips and cherries.

Spread in greased 9 x 5-inch loaf pan. Bake at 350° for 45 minutes or until done. Best if you let stand 24 hours before slicing.

Chocolate Caramel Pecan Rolls

*"Lavish sweet rolls with chips, pecans
and chocolate drizzled on top."*

Makes 1 Dozen

3 to 3½ cups sifted flour	
¼	cup sugar
1	teaspoon salt
1	package active dry yeast
1	cup water
2	tablespoons butter or margarine
1	egg
½	cup semi-sweet chocolate chips
2	tablespoons butter
½	cup chopped pecans

In a large bowl, combine 1½ cups flour, sugar, salt and yeast. Heat water and 2 tablespoons butter until hot (120–130°F). Add water mixture and egg to flour mixture and blend at low speed just until mixed. Continue mixing at high speed for 3 minutes. Stir in as much remaining flour as you can until dough pulls cleanly away from sides of bowl.

On floured surface, knead about 2 minutes. Roll dough into a 15 x 7-inch rectangle. Melt chocolate chips and 2 tablespoons butter together; cool and spread over rectangle. Sprinkle with

continued

pecans. Starting with long side, roll dough up jelly-roll fashion. Cut into 12 slices.

Sprinkle a greased 13 x 9-inch pan with Topping ingredients. Place dough slices on top. Cover loosely with plastic wrap or a towel. Let rise in warm place until nearly double (35 to 40 minutes). Bake at 375° for 25 to 30 minutes; turn out onto serving platter. If desired, drizzle Chocolate Glaze over the top of rolls.

Topping

½   cup brown sugar
¼   cup chopped pecans
½   cup butter or margarine, softened
2   tablespoons corn syrup

In a small bowl, combine all topping ingredients and mix well.

Chocolate Glaze

⅓   cup semi-sweet chocolate chips
1   tablespoon butter

In a small saucepan, melt chocolate chips and butter over low heat. Drizzle chocolate mixture over rolls, after you have turned them out onto serving platter.

Cheesecake-Chip
Sweet Rolls

*"Discover a new tradition to serve your guests
at breakfast or brunch."*

Makes 2½ Dozen

Sweet Roll Dough (see Glazed Orange 'N Chip Rolls)

Cheesecake Filling

6	ounces cream cheese, softened
½	cup sour cream
¼	cup sugar
2	tablespoons flour
2	teaspoons lemon juice
½	teaspoon vanilla
2	egg whites
1	cup semi-sweet chocolate mini-chips

Prepare sweet roll dough. Divide dough into 30 balls. Place balls 3 inches apart on greased cookie sheets. Pat each ball down into a round. Let rise until double, about 1 hour.

Mix filling ingredients (except chips) together in a mixing bowl and beat until smooth. With thumb make a 1½-inch indentation in center of each roll. Fill with cream cheese

continued

mixture. Sprinkle chips over filling. Bake at 375° for 10 to 15 minutes until golden brown. Cool and frost with Glaze.

Glaze

4 cups sifted powdered sugar
2 tablespoons butter, softened
1 teaspoon vanilla
6 to 10 tablespoons milk

Mix powdered sugar, butter and vanilla together. Add milk, a tablespoon at a time, beating until smooth and creamy.

Hint: You can make 1 batch of Sweet Roll Dough and divide it in half. Make ½ the filling for Cheesecake Chip Sweet Rolls and ½ the filling for Orange 'N Chip Rolls. Follow directions on recipe.

Glazed Orange 'N Chip Rolls

"The wonderful fragrance of orange and chocolate fills the kitchen as these bake."

Makes 2 Dozen

Sweet Roll Dough

1	package active dry yeast
¼	cup warm water
½	cup sugar
¾	cup milk, scalded
1	teaspoon salt
2	eggs, beaten
4	cups all-purpose flour or bread flour
½	cup butter, melted

Soften yeast in water with ½ teaspoon of the sugar. Let stand 10 minutes. In a saucepan, scald milk and add remaining sugar and salt to it. Cool and add softened yeast, mixing well. Add eggs and half the flour, blending until smooth. Beat in cooled butter and the remaining flour until thoroughly mixed. Cover dough and let set 10 minutes before kneading.

Knead on floured board, until smooth and elastic (about 10 minutes). Do not add more than ¼ cup more flour for

continued

kneading. The dough must be soft, too much flour makes the rolls too bread-like. Place kneaded dough in a greased bowl, turn once to bring greased side to top. Cover with waxed paper and let rise until doubled. Punch down and shape into rolls (see directions under filling).

Orange-Chip Filling

¼	cup butter, softened
½	cup sugar
2	tablespoons grated orange peel
1	cup semi-sweet chocolate mini-chips

After dough is punched down, roll into 2 (17 x 12-inch) rectangles. Spread with softened butter. Mix sugar, orange peel and chips together and sprinkle over top. Starting with long side, roll dough up jelly-roll fashion, tucking in ends.

Cut each roll into 12 slices and place in 2 greased 9 x 13-inch pans. Cover and let rise until double, about 1 hour. Bake at 375° for 12 to 15 minutes until golden brown. While hot, frost with Orange Glaze and remove to wire racks to cool.

Orange Glaze

1	cup sifted powdered sugar
2	teaspoons grated orange peel
2 to 3	tablespoons orange juice

Beat powdered sugar, orange peel and orange juice in a mixing bowl until smooth and creamy.

Coconut and Chocolate Swirl Rolls

"These rolls came right from heaven!"

Makes 16 Rolls

Rolls

⅓	cup milk
6	tablespoons unsalted butter
½	cup cream of coconut (Coco Casa)
1	teaspoon vanilla
¾	teaspoon salt
3	large eggs
1	package dry yeast, dissolved in 2 tablespoons warm water
4	cups flour

Filling

3	tablespoons melted butter
¾	cup grated coconut
¾	cup semi-sweet chocolate mini-chips
¾	cup chopped toasted almonds or pecans

continued

Glaze

3	tablespoons butter, melted
2	cups sifted powdered sugar
3 to 4	tablespoons hot coffee
1	(1-ounce) square unsweetened chocolate or 1 teaspoon maple flavoring

In a saucepan, scald milk over low heat; stir in butter until melted. Add cream of coconut, vanilla and salt; set aside.

In a mixing bowl, beat eggs lightly and add milk mixture, yeast and flour. Knead until dough is pliable and satiny, adding more flour if necessary.

Place in a large buttered bowl. Cover with a piece of buttered aluminum foil. Let rise in a warm place until it triples in volume. Punch down and roll into a 16 x 7-inch rectangle.

Spread melted butter over dough. Combine the rest of filling ingredients and spread over butter. Starting with long side, roll up jelly-roll fashion. Pinch edges to seal. Cut roll into 16 pieces. Place in greased 13 x 9-inch pan.

Let dough rise again for 30 minutes to 1 hour until doubled. Bake at 375° for 20 minutes until golden brown. Combine Glaze ingredients; blend until smooth. Drizzle over hot rolls. Cool on racks.

Frosted Chocolate Doughnuts

"Hard to resist either glazed or chocolate frosted."

Makes 2 Dozen

2	eggs
1¼	cups sugar
¼	cup vegetable oil
1	teaspoon vanilla
4	cups flour (bread flour is best)
⅓	cup unsweetened cocoa powder
1	tablespoon plus 1 teaspoon baking powder
1	teaspoon ground cinnamon
¾	teaspoon salt
¼	tcaspoon baking soda
¾	cup buttermilk

In a mixing bowl, beat eggs well. Gradually add sugar, beating until thick and lemon colored. Blend in oil and vanilla. Mix the next six ingredients together and add to batter alternately with buttermilk. Cover and chill several hours.

Take half of dough and roll out to ½-inch thickness on lightly floured surface. Cut with doughnut cutter and fry in hot oil (375°) for 1 minute until golden. Turn and cook about 1 more minute. Drain on paper towels and dip top in glaze or frost with chocolate frosting. If desired, decorate doughnuts with nuts or sprinkles.

continued

Glaze

4	cups sifted powdered sugar
½	teaspoon cinnamon
1	teaspoon vanilla
¼	cup plus 2 tablespoons milk
	Chopped nuts, optional
	Sprinkles, optional

Mix powdered sugar, cinnamon, vanilla and milk until smooth. Glaze or frost cooled doughnuts and decorate with nuts or sprinkles.

Chocolate Frosting

4	(1-ounce) squares unsweetened chocolate
2	egg whites
1½	cups powdered sugar
1	cup butter, softened

Melt chocolate in double boiler; set aside. Beat egg whites until stiff; gradually add powdered sugar. Beat in butter and chocolate until creamy. Frost cooled doughnuts.

Chocolate French Toast

"For a special breakfast or brunch."

Makes 4 to 5 Servings

2	bars (1.45 ounces each) milk chocolate
16	(½-inch thick) diagonally cut slices from a long French bread
3	eggs
¾	cup chocolate milk
	Pinch cinnamon or nutmeg
2	tablespoons butter
1	tablespoon vegetable oil
	Powdered sugar

Break each chocolate bar into 4 equal rectangles. Sandwich each piece between 2 slices bread. In a shallow dish, beat eggs, milk and nutmeg with a fork. Soak each sandwich in egg mixture (30 seconds per side).

In a large, heavy skillet, heat butter and oil over medium-low heat. Cook until golden brown. Drain on paper towel and sprinkle with powdered sugar. Serve with fresh fruit.

Chocolate was only a drink until 1875. In Switzerland, Daniel Peter invented a way to make milk chocolate that could be melted to be eaten as candy.

Chocolate Chocolate Chip Dessert Waffles

"Top with whipped cream or your favorite ice cream."

Makes 4 cups batter

2	eggs, room temperature
¼	cup butter, melted
1	teaspoon vanilla
1	cup buttermilk or sour milk
1	cup flour, sifted
¾	cup sugar
½	cup unsweetened cocoa powder
½	teaspoon baking powder
½	teaspoon baking soda
¼	teaspoon salt
¼	teaspoon cinnamon
¾	cup chopped pecans or walnuts
½	cup semi-sweet chocolate mini-chips
⅓	cup peanut butter chips (optional)

Preheat waffle iron. In a mixing bowl, beat eggs, butter and vanilla until light and fluffy. Mix in buttermilk; gradually add flour, sugar, cocoa, baking powder, baking soda, salt and cinnamon.

Mix well and stir in nuts and chips. Bake waffles and serve immediately with your favorite topping.

Beverages

Chocolate Chocolate Malt

"So good, it's like a weekend—never lasts long enough!"

Makes 2 Servings

¼   cup regular or chocolate milk
2   tablespoons chocolate syrup
2   tablespoons instant chocolate malted milk
         powder
2   cups chocolate ice cream, softened
       Whipped cream, garnish
       Cookie, garnish

In a blender container mix milk, chocolate syrup and malted milk powder until blended. Add ice cream and blend until smooth. Pour into glasses and garnish with a dollop of whipped cream and a cookie wafer if desired.

Chocolate Devil

"A sinful, sensuous, dusky delight."

Makes 2 Servings

3	tablespoons Amaretto liqueur
3	tablespoons chocolate liqueur
2	cups chocolate ice cream
½	cup milk
3 to 4	ice cubes
	Dash of cinnamon, garnish (optional)
	Cinnamon stick, garnish (optional)
	Scoop of ice cream, garnish (optional)

In a blender, combine the Amaretto, chocolate liqueur, chocolate ice cream, milk and ice. Blend thoroughly and pour into 2 frosted (6 ounce) glasses.

Garnish with a dash of cinnamon and a cinnamon stick or add a scoop of your favorite ice cream.

Chocolate-Mint Soda

"A newly minted version of an old favorite."

Makes 4 Servings

½	cup chocolate syrup
¼	cup whipping cream, whipped
1¾	cups club soda
3	cups peppermint ice cream

In a large bowl, mix chocolate syrup and whipped cream together. Stir in club soda until foamy. Mix in ice cream and stir until blended. Pour into glasses and serve with a straw.

Chocolate's history is as rich in lore as the wonderful flavor of the cocao bean itself. The Spanish conquerors found the beans being used as money in Mexico.

Chocolate Milk Punch

"Such a soothing combination of milk, chocolate and spirits."

Makes 1 Serving

1	cup cold milk
2	tablespoons chocolate syrup
1	jigger bourbon
2	tablespoons crushed ice
	Grated nutmeg, garnish

Blend milk, chocolate syrup, bourbon, and crushed ice in a blender. Blend until well mixed; serve with a sprinkle of grated nutmeg on top.

A fashionable chocolate drink was served in taverns and chocolate houses in Europe and the American colonies during the 1700's and 1800's. From a tavern sign in Massachusetts:

Francis Symonds makes and sells
The best of Chocolate, also Shells
I'll toll you if you need
And feed you well and bid you speed.

Chocolate Sting

"Ahhh."

Makes 1 Serving

1   ounce chocolate mint liqueur
         (Vandermint)
1   ounce brandy
         Crushed ice

Shake liqueur and brandy vigorously with ice. Strain into chilled cocktail glass.

Brown Belt

"It's the little things in life that count."

Makes 1 Serving

1   ounce dark creme de cacao
1   ounce vodka
         Crushed ice

Shake creme de cacao and vodka briskly with ice. Strain into a chilled cocktail glass.

Brandy Alexander

"Small cheer and great welcome makes a merry feast."
—William Shakespeare

Makes 1 Serving

1	ounce brandy
1	ounce creme de cacao
1	ounce cream
	Nutmeg or unsweetened cocoa powder, garnish

Shake brandy, creme de cacao and cream with ice. Strain into cocktail glass. Sprinkle with nutmeg or cocoa powder, if desired.

Alexander the Greatest

"A great combination of dessert and after dinner drink."

1	ounce dark creme de cocoa
1	ounce brandy
1	scoop vanilla ice cream
¼	cup finely chopped ice
	Unsweetened cocoa powder, garnish

Combine creme de cocoa, brandy, ice cream and ice in a blender. Blend until smooth. Pour into goblets and sprinkle with cocoa powder, if desired.

Mexican Hot Chocolate

"To be drunk from a golden goblet."

The ancient Aztecs and Toltecs considered chocolate a food of the gods, bestowed by the god Quetzalcoatl. Chocolate was prized and considered to be a source of strength, energy, wisdom and an aphrodisiac. They called it xoco-latl and it consisted of ground cocoa seeds, water, spices and ground vanilla pods. The mixture was worked into a thick paste and beaten until foamy.

This spicy chocolate foam was often eaten with a jeweled spoon or drunk from a golden goblet. Montezuma, the emperor, was said to have finished off fifty pitchers of xoco-latl a day!

Makes 4 Servings

3	tablespoons unsweetened cocoa powder
3	tablespoons sugar
½	cup water
1½	cups milk
1	egg
½	teaspoon vanilla
⅛	teaspoon cinnamon
	Dash ground cloves
	Dash freshly grated nutmeg

continued

Mix cocoa and sugar in heavy saucepan; gradually stir in water. Stir until cocoa is dissolved. Heat, stirring frequently, over medium heat until hot. Stir in milk; heat until very hot.

Meanwhile, whisk egg in small bowl until frothy; whisk in vanilla, cinnamon, cloves, and nutmeg. Continue whisking until light. Whisk egg mixture into hot cocoa mixture.

Whisk until frothy and serve immediately.

Spirited Chocolate Eggnog

"A chocolate love potion."

Makes 10 Servings

3	eggs, separated
2	tablespoons sugar
1	cup chocolate-flavored milk
¼	cup creme de cacao
¼	cup Amaretto
½	teaspoon vanilla
2	cups whipping cream
2	tablespoons sugar
	Ground nutmeg, garnish

In a mixing bowl, beat egg yolks until blended. Gradually add 2 tablespoons sugar and continue beating for 5 minutes until thick and lemon colored. Stir in milk, cream de cacao, Amaretto and vanilla until well blended. Cover and chill.

In a large bowl, beat whipping cream until soft peaks form; set aside. In another bowl, beat egg whites until soft peaks form; gradually add remaining 2 tablespoons sugar until stiff peaks form. Fold whipped cream and egg whites into chilled mixture. Serve immediately and sprinkle nutmeg over each serving.

Old-Fashioned Hot Chocolate

"Something chocolate to sip on that will warm you all up."

Makes 4 Servings

3	(1-ounce) squares unsweetened chocolate
½	cup sugar
	Dash salt
1	cup water
3	cups milk
	Whipped cream, garnish
	Cinnamon, garnish

In a saucepan, combine chocolate, sugar, salt and water. Cook over low heat, stirring constantly until chocolate melts.

Slowly stir in milk and heat until hot. Whisk or beat with rotary beater until foamy on top. Garnish, if desired, with whipped cream and cinnamon.

Chocolate was the royal drink of the Aztecs as well as the Incas of Peru. The Spanish explorer, Hernando Cortez, introduced chocolate as a hot beverage, sweetening it with cane sugar and vanilla.

Hot Mocha Mix

"Breathe in the chocolate fragrance of a steaming cupful."

Makes 12 Servings

1	cup unsweetened cocoa powder
2	cups sugar
2	cups nonfat dry milk powder
½	cup instant coffee
2	cups dry non-dairy coffee creamer
1	vanilla bean, cut in quarters

Mix all ingredients together. Pack in jars making sure each has a piece of bean.

Store in refrigerator at least one week before using. For each serving, use 3 tablespoons of mix. Add boiling water and stir.

Mocha mix can be kept indefinitely in tightly covered jar in refrigerator.

Café Au Cacao

"A tantilizing coffee flavor flirts with the fragrance of chocolate."

Makes 12 Cups

½   gallon cold coffee
½   gallon chocolate ice cream, softened
¾   cup dark creme de cacao
½   cup whipping cream
        Whipped cream, garnish
        Unsweetened cocoa powder, garnish

Combine coffee, ice cream and creme de cacao. Whip ½ cup whipping cream and gently fold into coffee mixture.

Pour into serving cups and garnish with a dollop of whipped cream and a sprinkle of cocoa powder.

Chocolate Creme Liqueur

"The ingredients aren't exotic but the result is out of this world."

Makes 4½ Cups

1	cup half and half cream
1	(14-ounce) can sweetened condensed milk
1	cup milk
2	teaspoons instant coffee crystals
1	egg yolk, beaten
1	cup Irish Whiskey
⅓	cup rum
1	tablespoon chocolate extract
1	tablespoon vanilla

In a large heavy saucepan, combine cream, milks and coffee crystals. Cook and stir over medium heat until crystals dissolve. Stir some of the hot mixture into beaten egg yolk and gradually return mixture to saucepan. Bring to boil. Continue cooking over medium heat for 2 minutes. Remove from heat.

Stir in whiskey, rum, chocolate extract and vanilla; cool mixture. Pour into bottle or jar with tight fitting lid. Chill overnight and shake well before serving. Store in refrigerator for up to 2 months.

Index

Order Page

Additional copies of "Chocolate Mousse and Other Fabulous Chocolate Creations" can be ordered for $9.95 plus $1.50 for postage and handling, from:

The Branches
1389 Park Road
P.O. Box 848
Chanhassen, MN 55317

Other cookbooks available
through The Branches

Recipes From Minnesota With Love (by Betty M. Potter) 9.95
Winning Recipes From Minnesota With Love 9.95
Winning Recipes From Wisconsin With Love 9.95
Recipes From Arizona With Love 9.95
Recipes From Iowa With Love 9.95
Winning Recipes From South Dakota With Love 9.95
Recipes From Maine With Love 9.95
Recipes From Missouri With Love 9.95
The Just For Kids Cookbook (by Betty M. Potter) 9.95
The Just For Kids Apron 9.00

Make checks payable to: The Branches
1389 Park Road
P.O. Box 848
Chanhassen, MN 55317

**Add $1.50 for postage and handling on first item,
$ .50 for additional items on the same order.**

Order Page

Now that you are an official "Mousse Club" member as the owner of this cookbook, you can also "look" official with these accessory items. We can't guarantee they will improve your cooking, but they will definitely add to the fun!

Official "Mousse Club" Apron $12.00

High quality full size (30") apron done in tasteful light chocolate with dark chocolate color trim. Of course, the official "Mousse Club" insignia is permanently and prominently displayed on the bib.

Official "Mousse Club" Mug $6.00

11 oz. ceramic mug with insignia permanently displayed.

Official "Mousse Club" Hot Pad $5.00

Matching partner to the apron in both colors and quality, with the insignia screened on one side. The perfect item for those hot chocolate recipes.

Add $1.50 for postage and handling on first item,
$ .50 for additional items on the same order.

MOUSSE

CHOCOLATE · INTERNATIONAL · CLUB

©NEW BOUNDARY DESIGNS 1986

OFFICIAL "MOUSSE CLUB" INSIGNIA